From Beach Hut to Palace

A story of church repurposed

JAMES GALLOWAY

RIVER

PUBLISHING

River Publishing & Media Ltd
Barham Court
Teston
Maidstone
Kent
ME18 5BZ
United Kingdom

info@river-publishing.co.uk

All Scripture quotations are taken from the New International Version © 1978 New York International Bible Society, published in the UK by Hodder & Stoughton.

ISBN 978-1-908393-00-5

Printed in the United Kingdom

Contents

**Dedicated to
the next generation**

Acknowledgements

With thanks...

To Jesus, who continually fulfils His promise to build His Church.
To Becky and our two boys. I love you! Who'd have thought...
To Team BCC. You rock my world and are shaking a city to its core!
To our friends around the world who continue to champion us on.
To our pastor friends who have invested and encouraged us throughout this epic journey.
To Jonathan Bugden, who told me to write this book.
To Steffy, my PA, who worked tirelessly, skilfully and patiently, from start to finish on this project.
To Tim Pettingale, who so believed and encouraged us in the writing of this book.
To my friends and family at Breathe City Church.
#WeAreBCC!

What Others Are Saying About This Book

"With clarity and passion, James Galloway relates the story of an intriguing and hope-filled leadership journey.

Some authors will wait until their story is near its end before writing, with glossy retrospection, about their achievements. This book is refreshingly different. It's about a great success still in the making. The signs are clearly there – this is a group of believers destined for something special. Yet there is no sense of triumphalism here, of having done it all. Instead, this is a very candid look at the real, ongoing challenges and opportunities presented by local church leadership.

If you too are on a leadership journey, you'll take from this book great encouragement in your own sense of destiny, plus clear forward-looking strategies for growth. Most of all, you will be inspired, knowing that God can do extraordinary things with the most raw of raw talent."

Mal Fletcher
2020 Plus & Next Wave International

"It has been a privilege to know and observe the development of James Galloway from a young schoolboy to a significant church leader. This book welcomes you into his heart and shares his learnings. It is an honest, vibrant and exciting adventure, not yet finished."

David Shearman
Senior Pastor, Christian Centre, Nottingham

"For BCCers this book is a milestone, an early marker post on a long adventure that is still to be fully realised. But for non-BCCers like me, who have grown to appreciate James Galloway's unassuming passion to build a thriving church in Stoke, it is revelatory.

I now fully understand what all the fuss was about! And I empathise from our parallel journey of reinventing and repurposing church in Bradford.

This book is like BCC: radical, edgy, passionate, insightful and totally Jesus-centred. It should not be copied as a formula, but rather offers leadership principles and encouragement to simply say 'yes' to God as He leads you to build a radical expression of His church where you live."

Stephen Matthew
Senior Associate Pastor, Abundant Life Church, Bradford

"Scripture is the narrative of God's love for humanity - 'story' is the foundation of the teachings of Jesus - and in this tradition James Galloway tells his stunning story of despair to vitality and the growth of the church, BCC.

James as a wise storyteller lets the voice of many changed lives fill this book, alongside his own journey of repurposing and repositioning the church. You will be encouraged, inspired, maybe even infuriated, but you won't walk away from these pages left to continue on unchallenged. James is a fresh and necessary voice in the English Church world. I recommend your time and energy. Don't put this book on a shelf – give it to someone hungry for change and adventure."

Simon McIntyre
Board of Directors, C3 Global

"Repurposing church is a critical contribution to the reformation of the Church in the Western world. For those who are not fully satisfied with an attractional model of church, this book is for you. Pain, prayer and dying to self that results in transformation is the end result of this deeply moving journey. Read it at your own risk. You may like it or hate it. But you cannot ignore what takes place when deep care for your community overtakes political correctness."

Ian Green

Leader & Founder, Next Level International

"I don't know of a place where people LOVE their church like BCC. The story of Breathe City Church gives us a roadmap for how bold leadership, big vision and passionate love for God and for people can transform a community. If it can happen in Stoke, it can happen where you and me are. Beware – after reading this, you might want to become a BCCer too!"

Anthony Delaney

Lead Pastor, Ivy Church, Manchester

"BCC is a VERY cheeky church. It's filled with the kind of faith that tears off the roof so that lives can be radically transformed by the power of Jesus Christ. This book tells the story of the past three and half years of journeying. It's inspiring, honest and even a bit controversial at times. But at the heart of it is raw passion – and an irrepressible belief that a city will be saved!

Well ... imagine if that was to happen in the heart of every church. A whole nation could be saved!"

Roy Todd

Lead Pastor, J24 Church, Nottingham

"Refreshingly honest, authentic, challenging and truly inspiring! *From Beach Hut to Palace* is a clear call from Pastors James and Becky Galloway to build strong churches that will shake this nation and the nations with the love of God.

James and Becky are great leaders with a massive heart for people. We need strong UK churches that are led by courageous leaders. Read this book and be stirred into action!

If you are tired of the 'same old, same old' then I urge you to read this book and become a world changer!"

John Greenow
Lead Pastor, Xcel Church

"Stoke on Trent is in transformation. For the last decade the city has battled to regenerate and the local church has been galvanised by the Spirit of God to arise and contend for the people and the land. It had been an inspiring and progressive journey thus far at a consistent, familiar pace, when James and Becky Galloway were planted by God into our midst. The Formula 1 acceleration of their local church model was a surprise that reverberated across the city. As they totally repurposed a congregation into one of the most influential churches in the area, their vision and action brought a quality provocation that challenged mindsets and tested hearts across the city.

Who they are and how they walk/run will provoke you to re-evaluate how *you* see church. There are many gems within this book, born from the crucible of experience. 'It is the glory of kings to search a matter out' - go find them!"

Jonathan Bellamy
CEO, Cross Rhythms

"Pioneering, adventurous and off the beaten track only just begins to describe the heart and spirit of James Galloway and Breathe City Church. This is just the beginning of a very exciting journey of lives in a city being transformed with dynamic faith and unfailing love. Let yourself be challenged and inspired to go beyond what you've known - step into what God can do!"

Clive Urquhart
Senior Pastor, Kingdom Faith Church

"I highly recommend you to take the time to read this book. You will certainly be inspired to think outside of the box when it comes to growing a healthy church. There's no shortage of opinions around today, but in this book are the words of a man and a church that have dared to move beyond mere theory and opinion to being successful practitioners.

This book contains many great lessons and nuggets from a church that has an incredible tale of multi-site growth which is an ongoing tale. A very good read that will both inspire you to think differently and give you tools to go for it yourself!"

Andy Elmes

Senior Leader, Family Church & Synergy Churches

"I believe that it's too early to write this book. Surely one needs to wait for the cement to dry before opening the doors for a grand inspection? In it, James Galloway claims to have broken the 80:20 rule that states that 80% of the workload, finances, prayers and energy comes from only 20% of the people. He obviously hasn't read the manual – the 80:20 rule is a *rule*, not a mild suggestion! James also calls what's been created in Stoke on Trent a 'Palace'. Doesn't that break the golden rule of humility? Surely we, the Inspectors, should make that claim, not him!

What is BCC?

Who is James Galloway?

What is all the hullabaloo?

This book doesn't just explain the story, it is the story – out of time, out of place and out from nowhere. Much like Gary Numan when he appeared on the world stage with the first fruits of Electro-pop in the 80s. It was unnerving, before its time, ground breaking, innovative, exciting, yet misunderstood.

Isn't that how all great things begin?"

Dave Gilpin

Senior Pastor, Hope City Church

Preface: The Conversation of Change

In the summer of 2007 my family and I went to a beach hut in Somerset for three weeks. We went not out of choice or desire, but because we were broken, confused, disappointed and desperate. Becky, my wife, had confided in her parents, who are wonderful people, and they arranged and paid for us to spend the summer in a hut no bigger than a shed on a beach. It had a view of the city where we had resigned ministry and knew we were leaving. After 13 years of effort, to walk away into the unknown was a terrifying experience.

What happened in those three weeks can only be described as a miraculous healing. As part of that process we also received a heavenly "download" of the church that God was mandating us to build. We weren't 100% sure about the location, but it seemed like we might be heading to my home city of Stoke on Trent.

On 2nd September 2007, we drove away from that beach hut.

Today, 8th December 2010, I'm back in the same beach hut writing about a palace, a temple, a house of God that has been built in Stoke on Trent, my home city, where we have the privilege of being lead pastors. *From Beach Hut to Palace* is a story of repurposing church and allowing the audacious, eccentric passion of Jesus, with His commitment to build His church to overcome any obstacle that may be placed in its way.

My desire is that the pages of this book give you the essence of the immense journey that God has taken Becky, our boys and myself, and

Breathe City Church on during the last three and a half years. It is less of a strategic, hardwired manual and more of a heart journey – an emotional conveyance of a transformation that we are all absolutely humbled to be a part of.

I may never know precisely what the Holy Spirit did in those three weeks in the summer of 2007. I'm pretty sure that I may never need to know. I have come to a place where I am confident that it is okay to live with unanswered questions and am pretty happy to not be in control of what lies ahead. People laugh when they hear me say that in the summer of 2007, I died. I am evidently grasping the revelation that Paul also experienced when he uttered these elaborate words:

"Since we have died … how can we continue to live … we were joined with Christ in baptism, we joined with him in his death … For we died and were buried in Christ by baptism. And just as Christ was raised from the dead by the glorious power of the Father, now we may also live new lives." (Romans 6:2-4)

I will always give God praise for what He did from that day to this. I may never understand it or even claim to have instigated it, but history declares that this time has existed and that God has accomplished infinitely more than one may ask or even imagine (Ephesians 3:20). I will be forever amazed and will continue to brag on the phenomenal God we serve and the energetic and passionate church that we are privileged to lead.

There may be better books to read that will help you, in instructional form, to repurpose church, but this book is designed to give a brief glimpse into the heartbeat and feeling of what it feels like to repurpose church. It is a testimony that Jesus is still building His Church:

"I will put together my church, a church so expansive with energy that not even the gates of hell will be able to keep it out." (Matthew 16:18 MSG)

This is a glimpse into what can happen when people say, "Yes" to their God.

From Beach Hut to Palace – A story of church repurposed.

My Prayer...

As you read this book, this is my prayer:

That this story would be an inspiration to all who read it. That the testimonies contained within would encourage many a person and leader to re-engage with the challenge that every generation faces: to stand on the shoulders of giants and build with those who will come after us in mind.

My prayer is that Breathe City Church continues to go from strength to strength and that our city is reached by real people being used by a real God. My prayer is that this extravagant message of faith, hope and love that the Church carries will be communicated in such a way that this generation can hear it.

My prayer is a thank you from the very depths of who I am for the privileged part that I get to play in Your global, multi-generational "Plan A" called the Church! My prayer is one of gratitude and over-whelming humility that You chose us for such a time as this.

My prayer is that we would all fall more in love with You, Jesus, and that the Church we represent would shine bright in the cities and communities in which we serve.

My prayer is that God would be glorified and that you, the reader, would enjoy our story.

PART 1
THE
CONVERSATION
OF
CHANGE

This is a glimpse into what can happen when people say, "Yes" to their God...

INTRODUCTION

Yesterday, nearly 600 people gathered in multiple sites across the city of Stoke on Trent. Collectively, they are known as *Breathe City Church* (BCC). Individually, they call themselves "BCCers". This church is adventurous, radical, eccentric and even dangerous in its pursuit of Jesus and its passion for reaching the city.

Yesterday, I was told of a BCCer who is six days into detox, enduring the process of escaping the claws of heroin. Six months ago this beautiful young lady met Jesus for the first time. This princess and her young son have had their world turned upside down by the wonderful, gracious, dynamic power of the gospel. She and her son walked into BCC's *Campus: Meir* six months ago and now they walk with Jesus.

Yesterday, I spoke to a BCCer who two months ago, at an Alpha course that our Welcome Pastors run three times a year at our Campus: City, met Jesus for the first time and is now relearning how to live, walking with Jesus. He told me how, the night before, he was feeling randy and several ex-girlfriends were "coincidentally" sending him texts a plenty, offering to pay him a visit to help him with his present predicament. This young man, committed to following Jesus, remembered our Executive Pastor's advice: "Simply open the Word and God will help in testing times." The young man flicked open his pristine new Bible to Songs of Songs and declared, "This is worse than the stuff on the telly!"

Yesterday, I sat humbled as I took diligent notes during the meeting on the front row of our City Gathering. Behind me was a young mum who, two and a half years ago, had all her dreams come true when her young husband chose to follow Jesus. We both, along with several hundred people sat mesmerised as this young man, a BCCer, opened the Scriptures and spoke with the maturity of a preacher of 20 years or more.

Today, I sit at a desk in a beach hut in Somerset with my iPad, a hot mug of coffee, my Bible and journal, looking over the Bristol Channel with Cardiff on the horizon. Today I realise again that three and half years ago BCC didn't exist. Well, I say that, but I am very aware that BCC did exist in my heart and in the plans of God, but the stories above were a mere figment of my imagination.

I had heard stories of dynamic churches being planted and established. I had worked tirelessly with young people across South Wales and yet I never imagined what God would do in such a short space of time. Three and a half years ago I was over there, Cardiff – stuck, frustrated, insecure, being strangled by the perceived lack of progress and not realising what the future held.

In three and a half years I have been on an absolutely awesome adventure during which I have seen a sensational church built against all odds and immense opposition in a city that is often deemed the worst city in the nation – and all to my total amazement. Three and a half years ago I would never, in my wildest dreams, have thought that I would be Lead Pastor of a mind-blowing, rule breaking, status quo smashing church called BCC in my home city of Stoke on Trent. Never would I have thought that the journey my family and I have been on would become a story that is inspiring so many and seeing literally thousands of people across my city be *loved for who they are and inspired to become all that they can be.*

This book is that story.

This book is the story of a church of 60 people in crisis, a young frustrated pastor and his family, and the divine purposes of God colliding in a cataclysmic explosion of epic proportions, giving hope that Jesus *is* still building *His* Church in the 21st Century. This story is not a model of repurposing church or a blueprint of best practice. It is a simple tale, a testimony of how God in *His* timing and *His* choice can take hold of a group of people who are desperate and dead enough to dare to believe that the impossible is possible. It is about those who are brave enough to obey the leading of the Holy Spirit, against all opinion and history, and are now living the dream of building and experiencing great church in a great city.

This book is a testimony, or even a case study of a church walking through (some may say being dragged through) the process of being repurposed. It is evidence that past generations do have a legacy that can be built on. It is proof that the efforts of *yesterday*, if *today* is prepared to change, can be harnessed to shape *tomorrow*. It is a demonstration that that which went before doesn't have to be merely remembered, but can be stood upon by those brave enough to ask the difficult questions and stand by the answers that come.

Tomorrow, I will look back at what I've written. I may have a more mature and wise understanding of the journey, but I long for the passion, enthusiasm and emotion of today and for this story to be conveyed to you, the reader, in such a way that it will bring some revelation, inspiration, information and, dare I be so bold, even impartation.

Tomorrow, I will read this book with the added inserts of personal stories of BCCers who have also journeyed on this crazy adventure. Their stories are included to give a multi-dimensional view of the experience of repurposing church. Their stories are, as is mine, an honest account of what it is like to experience having everything one once regarded "normal" turned completely upside down and to now live the most exciting, dynamic and exhilarating life ever.

Tomorrow, I hope to read more stories of Jesus building *His* church in the 21st Century.

A BCC STORY: MANDY

The last three and a half years have been like a whirlwind. I have
never been so encouraged and enthusiastic about my
relationship with Jesus!
I realise now that this is how it should always be, but I was truly
unaware of how exciting it could be! Living the abundant life is true!
Looking back, I see that God has given me the desires of my heart
without me realising what they even were.
Being part of BCC is the best. It's a bunch of people who have a
desire to demonstrate the gospel in a real and life-changing way. I
love the way that the leadership has a clear direction
and will not be compromised.
What I have found most rewarding and an absolute joy is seeing
lives given to the Lord and having the privilege of being a part of
individuals' stories. God is so good!
I am much inspired by my time at BCC. I have never enjoyed
myself so much! Pastor James quotes the Psalm,
"We are the pen in the hand of a ready writer."
I feel I am in God's will and living the plan that He has
had for me all along. I am truly blessed
and consider it an honour to be
at BCC for such a time as this.
I wonder what will happen next? But God has got His plan
and if God knows, then that's good enough for me.

A BCC STORY: LAURA

Christmas 2007 saw a girl in her mid-twenties, far from God,
desperate, sad, empty and pretty much set to self-destruct.
Now, everyday, I thank God that she was seeking something more.
As close as she was to rock bottom, in the empty, hollow
pain that was never going to be healed by pills, the deluded promise
of a library of self-help books or well-intentioned but misguided
therapy, she was not quite ready to give up on life.
That girl found Alpha, found BCC and found God.
That girl came home.
That girl is proud to call herself a daughter of the house.
That girl is a born and bred BCCer.
That girl is me.
Count me as a changed life. Consider me a BCC success story.
Changed, rescued, healed – a life restored, no longer hindered
by past mindsets; free to live the life that God has chosen for
me. Consider me privileged to have a part to play in the story of
an awesome house of God being built in my home city, serving
phenomenal senior pastors,
alongside mighty men and women of God.
I am so grateful to all BCCers who have shared my journey so far,
who are committed to loving, inspiring, stretching, developing and
challenging me to be all that I can be. They have been there to share
tears and laughter, heartache and joy, as God shapes me into the
woman He always intended me to be.

THE CHAPTER BEFORE

Breathe City Church, with its explosive introduction and growth, has been described by some as an overnight success. There is much talk of the "mushroom syndrome" that we all recognise: here in a day and gone the next. In order to put the story of BCC into context, one has to understand that any given "overnight success" is built upon decades of preparation. I use the word "success" carefully. As I'm sure you would agree, in global terms there are far grander stories than BCC. However, in the present spiritual climate of the UK, to see 70% of church growth coming from first time decisions, one can clearly see that God is doing something!

The decades of preparation began in my home city of Stoke on Trent, seeing my parents re-encounter God at Emmanuel Hall in Biddulph. After only a few short years they took over a small church in a town called Wirksworth, Derbyshire. Teenage memories are always decorated with elaborate spin but I have, in the corners of my mind, the memory that the church had progressive growth and vague images that lead me to believe that the church moved from a difficult past to a healthy place in a period of eight years.

After dropping out of church for a couple of years, I had a dramatic encounter with God, aged 19, and instantly worked towards attending a Leadership Training School run by the Christian Centre, Nottingham – a great church led by Pastor David Shearman. I now realise that much of what I understand of leadership and building church stems from David and this great house of God.

I then moved to Cardiff where my parents were planting a church. This is where I met my wife, Becky, who was brought up in a great Anglican church with a long history. It was here, in a church-planting environment, that Becky and I began to realise that much of the legacy of past generations was not built upon when planting new churches. It was a revelation, primarily carried by Becky, that led us to a place of realisation: *if we could utilise the facilities and mantles of past generations and, at the same time, create a planting/pioneering atmosphere, we could achieve the best of both worlds.*

Church plants always tend to struggle with finances, facilities and establishing themselves with deep roots. In the 13 years of being in Cardiff, the church we were a part of moved from place to place and never fully established any roots. People say that buildings don't matter and that church is the people, but that is usually said by leaders who have great buildings. Pioneering is a hard slog: setting up and packing down every week for church, finding offices, generally working from home, carrying the financial burden of immense rental agreements on facilities that are not purpose-built, having to build plans around available facilities and every so often relocating...

As we were helping in this pioneering endeavour we watched church buildings worth millions of pounds being closed or sold off to be used as carpet warehouses or restaurants or trendy apartments. We watched the great roots that the Church had in the last generation being lost, because tradition was more important than empowering the next generation. The challenge was to develop a way of inheriting the great exploits of the past and the audacious spirit of the pioneer in order to create a process of bringing the past and the future together today.

In anyone's imagination such a possibility would create tension, but if that tension could be harnessed, imagine the possibilities. Considering the scenario logically, I can think of many of the apparently valid reasons why churches and organisations shy away from repurposing themselves. In general, it is safer, more comfortable and less offen-sive to stay away from change. But in the opinion of today, tomorrow is crying out for people to front up and grab change by the scruff of the neck and lead the way.

In 2 Kings 2, the story of Elijah and Elisha demonstrates the need to engage in a more demanding response *and* action. Elisha, repre-senting the next generation, asks to inherit a "double portion" and (please hear this) the opportunity to become Elijah's "successor". In order for Elisha to become Elijah's successor, Elisha had to *see* Elijah *taken*. I am persuaded that, currently, we don't model the passing on of a spiritual mantle for a church, a city or even a nation very well at all. Thus the next generation fails to pick up the mantle (cloak) and become *successors*.

David Shearman would very often say, "You have never succeeded until you have been succeeded." It is my belief that we fail the former generation and the coming generation if we refuse to address the issue of change or *repurposing* or *redefining*. Call it what you will, it is imperative that we wrestle with this issue so that the next genera-tion doesn't have to start again, but gets a head start and a "double portion".

A few years ago, on the new £1 coin and in the lyrics of an Oasis song, a famous quotation was rebirthed to a generation. I believe this was a prophetic urge to the Church to face the challenge of change:

Standing on the shoulders of giants.

Before my family and I moved to Stoke on Trent our "chapter be-fore" very much involved us watching, serving and discovering the hidden gems of the past generations. We honour those who went before us. However, one of the great Pentecostal pioneers, George Oldershaw, said it best when he uttered these great words:

Hats of to the past, coats off to the future.

When beginning a journey of repurposing change, the past must be honoured but not held sacrosanct. The future *must* be the deter-mining factor on all decisions and actions. The management of this will always be tricky and preventing collateral damage will be pretty much impossible. But for the kingdom's advancement and the salvation of the next generation, the brave must arise.

This immense challenge is why there are so many new church plants. I believe totally in church planting. Absolutely. I merely ask the question, "Can we plant churches utilising the legacy of the past, rather that letting it drop to the ground?"

Can an existing church be repurposed?

F.O.D. WALK

Some time ago I watched a documentary on TV. I had come home late and was channel flicking. What grabbed my attention on one channel was a line of air force staff marching in sync on the deck of an aircraft carrier. They were walking together looking at the floor, searching for evidence of any debris that might prevent the take off of any of their jets. Apparently this is known as the FOD walk.

Foreign Object Detection Walk

As soon as I heard this new piece of information something jumped in my spirit. I wanted to examine, by walking through Scripture and history, the church we had now become lead pastors of to see what I could discover. I had to ensure that nothing would prevent the "taking off" of what God was going to do.

[BETH uhl] (House of God)

We were now at Bethel Christian Church and Centre in Stoke on Trent, known by all around simply as "The Bethel".

Scholars inform me that Bethel is a city of Palestine about 19 kilometres (12 miles) north of Jerusalem. Bethel is first mentioned in the Bible in connection with the patriarch Abraham who,

"...pitched his tent with Bethel on the west and ... built an altar to the Lord." (Genesis 12:8; 13:3)

The region around Bethel is still suitable for grazing livestock. I thought that was interesting.

Jacob, Abraham's grandson, had a life-changing experience at this site. He had a vision of a staircase reaching into the heavens with the angels of God, *"ascending and descending on it"* (Genesis 28:12).

Jacob called the name of that place Bethel meaning *"the house of God"* (Genesis 28:19).

He erected a pillar at Bethel to mark the spot of his vision (Genesis 28:22, 31:13). Jacob later built an altar at Bethel where he worshiped the Lord (Genesis 35:1-16).

During Israel's war with the Benjaminites in later years (Judges 20), the children of Israel suffered two disastrous defeats (Judges 20:21,25). They went to Bethel to enquire of the Lord because the Ark of the Covenant was located there (Judges 20:26-27). At Bethel they built an altar and offered burnt offerings and peace offerings before the Lord. The third battle ended in disaster for the Benjaminites. At the end of the war the Israelites returned to Bethel, built an altar and again offered burnt offerings and peace offerings (Judges 21:1-4).

After the death of Solomon and the division of his kingdom, Jeroboam, the king of Israel (the northern kingdom) set up two calves of gold, one in Bethel and one in Dan (1 Kings 12:29, 32-33). Thus, Bethel became a great centre of idolatry (1 Kings 13:1-32, 2 Kings 10:29) and the chief sanctuary of Israel, rivalling the Temple in Jerusalem.

The prophets Jeremiah and Amos denounced Bethel for its idolatries (Jeremiah 48:13, Amos 5:5-6). Hosea, deploring its great wickedness (Hosea 10:5,15), called it Beth Aven (house of harlotry) because of the golden calf set up there. Bethel, the house of God, had deteriorated into Beth Aven, the house of harlotry.

In a religious reformation that sought to restore the true worship of God, King Josiah broke down the altar at Bethel (2 Kings 23:15). Still later in Israel's history, Bethel was occupied by Jewish people who returned from captivity in Babylon with Zerubbabel (Ezra 2:28, Nehemiah 7:32). The place again reverted to the Benjaminites (Nehemiah 11:31). The city was destroyed around 540 BC by a great fire.

This destruction may have been the work of Nabonidus of Babylon or of the Persians in the period just before Darius. Today, a small village called Beitin occupies the site of Bethel.

The New Testament does not refer to Bethel, but Jesus must have gone through this area on His trips. The city was situated on the main road from Shechem to Jerusalem.

"The Bethel"

After discovering all of this I went to the leadership team that I had inherited and presented my findings. I was bold and brash enough to say something along these lines:

"If Scripture is here for us to learn from, if we are Pentecostal people who believe in the prophetic, and if we want to ensure that history does not repeat itself, then we need to take note and act accordingly."

We all know and recognise that as leaders, we are to take responsibility for the position we find ourselves in and work towards our God-given destiny. Einstein states:

"The significant problems we face cannot be solved at the same level of thinking we were at when we created them."

It was evident and clear to me that the same level of thought and behaviour of the past would confine us to the same place we now found ourselves in. It was an obvious statement to make:

Things had to change in order for the next generation to be able to build upon something spectacular and not be at the same place we were in.

But it was upon these findings that immediate change began to occur and the journey of repurposing began.

A place called "Bethel" had God's attention again. His gaze was upon us. I was absolutely convinced that whatever the journey would cost, there was no way that God wanted Bethel to become another place where sheep could be grazed, but that *Breathe City Church* would become that "awesome place" spoken of in Genesis 28.

A BCC STORY: BAZ

The more I seem to know in any given subject area, the more
I realise I really don't know as much as I thought I did. Not too
long ago I would have said I had a fair knowledge and experience
of church. There may have been a few more things to learn and
experience, but these would have been minimal and gained
naturally over my lifetime.

So I thought.

Having witnessed a church begin to undergo the process of
repurposing under the direction of Pastors James and Becky,
I quickly found that the evaluations of my own knowledge and
understanding were rapidly decreasing and fading into
insignificance along with my ignorance.

The process of re-purposing church has, from my viewpoint,
taken me from a place of the ignorant belief that I was pretty much
up to speed with things, to the place where I now find myself
learning, growing and developing daily in the ways of a true
follower of Jesus and knowing that I will still be learning and
developing when I'm done here on earth.

To put it another way, I was bored and found church rather
mundane and uneventful. Now it changes and develops so fast and
with so much thrill and excitement that it pretty much consumes
most of my thoughts, most of the time.

A BCC STORY: DAVE

Who'd have thought a life could change so much in such
a short space of time, just by saying "Yes" to God?
On 8th August 2008 I said "Yes" to God and I thank Him that I was
able to say it in BCC. BCC was a church like I'd never experienced:
modern, lively, relevant and full of young people –
exactly where a new Christian should be.
BCC has a unique way of championing people, inspiring people,
loving people and catapulting them into their God-designed
futures. If someone had suggested a few years ago that
I would have preached God's Word in a church of hundreds,
I would have laughed it off. But the instant Pastor James
suggested it to me, I knew that I was being guided into my
calling. God has done some pretty awesome things in my life.
Due to the incredible church that BCC now is,
I have experienced so much in my short walk with God.
I have heard some of the greatest preachers on the planet,
received teaching that Jesus Himself would have been
proud to give and walked through doors that would not
have been open to me otherwise.
Through always saying "Yes" to God and being rooted in BCC,
my life has truly been transformed and I am seriously excited
about what else God has got in store for me and my family!
Thank you God, thank you BCC!

CERTAIN TO AWESOME

In any environment of repurposing church, that which went before us is essential. It is the starting point in discovering the foundations that we are building upon, inherited from yesterday; it is the legacy that we have at our disposal today and the vision of what is being built for tomorrow.

There is much conversation regarding culture from my generation, much of which needs to be realigned to Scripture rather than to preference or style. Understanding the importance of the word "Bethel" and attempting to ensure that what we were envisioning was according to Scripture, Genesis 28 took on a much greater level of importance not only for myself, but also for every BCCer. It is now the foundational understanding of who we are as a church. It also reveals, so strongly, our identity and culture as a house of God and it was the primary tool that we used to repurpose that which we inherited.

This passage of scripture helps to define what I believe BCC should look, smell, behave, sound, act and speak like. It is the epitome of any available vocabulary I have in regard to me clearly and prophetically understanding "church".

In this passage we read of Jacob, at sundown, setting up camp in a good place or a *certain* place according to differing translations.

That may not sound like anything dramatic or revelatory, until that is, one compares where Jacob wakes up. The passage of scripture goes on to inform the reader that when he awakes, Jacob describes the place formerly known as a good place or certain place, as an *awesome* place!

I recognise that I am no great scholar or theologian and I also admit to having an academic naivety, but according to my reckoning, Jacob wasn't transported anywhere like on *Star Trek* or another sci-fi movie. He was in the same place! What used to be a certain or good place was no longer that and is now itemised in the canon of Scripture as "an awesome place".

What changed? The place didn't for sure. So what did?

I accept that Jacob had a sensational, life-changing, amazing, movie-like dream. I can be fully persuaded that Jacob had an even greater thing than just a dream and actually experienced this dream as a reality. I'm sure that some could even build an argument to say that it was an "out of body experience" (I don't believe that it was, by the way). Yet nobody can argue that when he woke up, came around or returned to himself, that Jacob was not back in the same place...

...Yet it was different.

It was "an awesome place"!

It is my conviction and experience that many a church is a good church, even a certain church. But it is my understanding that the *"House of God, the very gateway to Heaven"* should be, as Jacob simply and passionately described it, an *awesome place* ...

...A place full of awe!

Awesome is defined as: "Inspiring awe or showing or characterised by awe".

This is the simple bedrock of what I believe church culture, design, expression, fragrance, speech, activity and effect should be like...

...AWESOME!

When people walk into our facilities, gatherings, functions and programmes; when people meet those who are part of the house of God, the people that Peter beautifully describes as *"living stones"* in 1 Peter 2:5, they should stand in awe. They should be amazed and have their minds shaken by what they see and hear, just like Jacob at this place he names *Bethel – the House of God.*

In understanding our inheritance, legacy and foundations it was clear that what we were to build for our tomorrows as Breathe City Church was to be AWESOME!

This clearly meant to me that mediocre, average, good, alright, okay and other descriptive words that compromised "awesome" had to be dealt with immediately. This was addressed by what we began to describe as our *Seven Cultural Pillars*. These came, as best as I can describe, as a download from heaven and their purpose was to "hold up" the very building of our future. These were more than fancy sermon titles, they were to be the fabric of *who we were to be*, individually and corporately.

Our cultural pillars were to be:

CLEAN: It was at this "awesome place" that Jacob began the process of cleaning up his life and dealing with some of his issues.

GENEROUS: Generosity is intrinsically linked to freedom. Jacob stopped life on the run and at this point began to give praise and give of himself!

HONOUR: Amazingly, Jacob recognised and honoured his past fathers' and God's ways.

POSITIVE: The place he occupied was the same, but Jacob's mindset saw it differently!

HEALTH: As in *all healthy things grow*. Jacob started afresh.

SECURE: A godly confidence was immediately downloaded to Jacob. He no longer lived scared.

TRUE: From this point, Jacob lived true and accurate to his divine destiny and purpose.

This revelation that totally transformed my world and my under-standing of church now had to be conveyed to the people.

This is where things got interesting.

The problem we have in church today is the volume of sermons we listen to – as in *we don't really listen!*

No matter how many times I tried to create sermons or build elaborate ways of communicating what I thought was great revelation, the spirit of mediocrity that said, "It's always been this way" wasn't budging. To be fair, I wasn't that patient and what I and a few accomplices did may not be recommended.

In 10 foot tall graffiti emblazoned across the auditorium of the church I had been leading for precisely one month, we painted the words "CERTAIN place" and "AWESOME place"!

Yes, you can imagine what happened.

Some people, when they walked in on Sunday morning, immediately turned around and left and others raised at least an eyebrow. Here we began our "cultural revolution" as the young, new pastor declared boldly and defiantly, "Church, we're moving from a certain place to an awesome place."

The journey of repurposing had begun.

PART 2
CULTURAL PILLARS

If the desired culture can be articulated clearly and
designed comprehensively then change is possible...

INTRODUCTION

Culture is defined as:

"The quality in a person or society that arises from a concern for what is regarded as excellent in arts, letters, manners, scholarly pursuits etc."

"A particular form or stage of civilisation, as that of a certain nation or period."

"The behaviours and beliefs characteristic of a particular social, ethnic or age group."

"Anthropology: the sum total ways of living built up by a group of human beings and transmitted from one generation to another."

Every organisation has a culture.

Fact.

Whether that organisation is a company, a sports club, a political party or a church, it has a culture.

In order to begin a process of redefining church for future generations, what must be understood is that culture is established by *default* or by *design*. Most culture in church life is established by default: "It's always been done like this..." etc. However, if the desired culture can be articulated clearly and designed comprehensively then change is possible.

The default setting will have to be challenged and reset by the design in hand.

Breathe City Church went through an 18 month wrestle between *default* and *designed* culture. The winner was designed culture.

It is possible.

BCC's culture is designed and defined by our seven Cultural Pillars: Clean, Generous, Honour, Positive, Health, Secure and True. They have been erected and established in order for designed culture to stand – in many cases in direct opposition to the default culture that was decades into its cultivation.

If a repurposing of church is to occur, then the desired *designed culture* has to be discovered, communicated, embraced and established.

Very often it would be considered that to change an organisation, structure is the primary focus of change. However, culture is the first thing that needs to be addressed for change to occur. A structure can change, but if culture doesn't change the church won't change.

So we began.

CULTURAL PILLARS: CLEAN

In this generation "clean" is not the most trendy or exciting conversation to have as a congregation of people! Maybe talk of a great vision of thousands of people coming together or taking a city for Jesus would attract more attention. In this generation of headlines, one could be forgiven for missing the detail.

Now I'm a headline type guy.

Even this book has been written in bite-size chunks, because my attention span is severely restricted!

Here's the deal: A CLEAN church is a HEADLINE.

Whilst playing golf with David Shearman, he began to explain the ingredients of a great church. Being a young, hungry leader, trying to glean from the great man, I ensured that I grasped hold of every sentence that was uttered during that round of golf. One sentence absolutely grabbed my attention: "A great church doesn't have lumpy carpets."

That line is the epitome of the culture of CLEAN.

Very often in church life, because of fear, lack of leadership, friendships or relational ties, we fail to deal with the issues at hand and find it easier to "sweep them under the carpet".

Since time and truth are friends, we will trip up on the lumpy carpet because, in time, truth always has its say.

In order for CLEAN to become a reality a few paradigm shifts have to occur.

The word "holy" in Greek is *hagiasmos* which means "set unto, given wholly over to and completely belonging to". Yet, there is so much associated baggage with being "holy" that there is a tendency to not discuss the subject in the 21st Century.

Let's break it down.

Mary & Martha

When we first arrived in Stoke on Trent, the church we inherited was in utter disarray. Immediately we had to deal with many, many practical issues, such as child protection, fire regulations, job descriptions, contracts and the like. However, there was a conversation held in every corner regarding our lack of spirituality and godliness, because our focus was similar to Martha and not, like our critics, similar to Mary.

It was thought that we should sit at the feet of Jesus and worship, pray and intercede, and that this would build a great church.

In Matthew, when we look at the feeding of the 5,000 men, plus women and children, who does Jesus commission with the job of feeding the people? Have a look:

Jesus says, *"You feed them."*

In the well-known passage that BCC commonly calls the "Matt 25 Challenge", have a look at the people who Jesus acknowledges.

It's the people that *do*.

Martha was the person who actually opened the door for Jesus to come into the house. Martha was the one who facilitated the hospitality of Jesus. If it wasn't for Martha's willingness to get down and *do* then this encounter they had with Jesus would not have occurred.

What Martha got wrong was that she was *distracted*. Holiness is not simply being like Mary and basking in the presence of Jesus all the time and it's also not being busy and distracted. We have to give Him our *whole attention*.

Don't beat yourself up

There is much effort made by wonderful and godly people who are trying to be like Jesus. We had to wade through the farcical "legal religiosity" that grips much of Christendom to help people gain a revelation of the wonderful journey of grace that we were embarking on. What helped most was the constant reading of Galatians 5:4 from several translations.

Read it.

And again.

And again.

I love how Eugene Peterson paraphrases it in The Message:

"I suspect that you would never intend this, but this is what happens. When you attempt to live by your own religious plans and projects you are totally cut off from Christ, you fall out of grace..."

In order to gain a more holistic understanding of what it is to be a CLEAN house we have to free people from the difficult burden they carry of trying to attain to the standard that all professional Christians falsely portray. In reality, we are all working out our salvation with fear and trembling (Philippians 2:12).

Holiness is not to do with a list of do's and don'ts or a separation from all unclean things. It is all about giving one's self totally over to God.

The word "holy" could be best read and understood as "wholly".

Completely.

100%.

There is "stuff" that we allow in our world that simply prevents us from being whole.

Complete.

100%.

What I felt strongly to do with the church, whilst this revelation was dawning on us, was to examine a few areas that in general prevent people from being whole.

Rebellion

I'm not saying here that we are all rebellious, nasty people. I'm sure we all genuinely love Jesus with all our hearts. I'm not talking about a traditional understanding of "sin".

I am talking about our choices.

I'm talking about when we hear that still small voice of prompting from the Holy Spirit, His Word or godly advice from others and we rebel by ignoring, saying, "No" or procrastinating.

Don't you just wish that this Christianity thing was an instant download? You know, like Mr. Anderson receives when he becomes Neo. That combat download just before he learns how to fight or the three second download that leads to him being able to fly a helicopter (if you're a fan of *The Matrix* you will be lost in your world of imagination right now... COME BACK!)

Learning to serve Jesus is not an instant download.

In fact, it's worse.

Jesus clearly instructed us to pick up our cross daily. All the self-help preaching in the 21st Century sure does make me feel good, but it isn't going to help me in reality, as I have to take responsibility for this walk and pick up my cross daily and follow Him.

Rebellion prevents this.

Don't rebel.

Pick it up daily.

Hurt

This is a tough one.

Honestly.

People everywhere resonate with this.

In the conversation between Jesus and Peter regarding whether Peter loves Jesus, have you ever noticed that Jesus hurt Peter? Or maybe we should say that Jesus' *questioning* hurt Peter?

People everywhere have been hurt – by people, situations, church and life. Here we see that even Peter is hurt by what Jesus said.

When Jesus teaches the disciples how to pray He says something absolutely outrageous that I'm pretty sure He got wrong. I mean He must have, right?

He says, *"Forgive us our sins, as we forgive those who have sinned against us..."*

Ouch.

Gets me every time.

I've got to forgive.

Hurt pervades many congregations because we are not able to step into healing, since we haven't forgiven.

Let go.

Forgive.

As the phrase goes, "Hurt people, hurt people. Whole people, heal people".

For the house to be CLEAN a change of thinking had to be achieved. Firstly, we had to rearrange our understanding that holiness is not about a bunch of do's and don'ts. Then we had to start building WHOLE people who are YES people and FORGIVING people.

CULTURAL PILLARS: GENEROUS

The culture of generosity is one that is easily identifiable, often talked about and yet very difficult to engineer.

And a culture of generosity is the easiest aspect to lose of any church or organisation.

The culture of generosity needs consistent work.

Why?

Generosity stares the "gospel of ME" direct in the face and challenges it daily.

Generosity is selfless in a selfish world and is absolutely counter cultural. It picks a fight with self, poverty mindsets, victim mindsets, greed, safety, comfort and many of the established cultural giants of our communities.

Generosity is so Jesus!

The process of walking a church through repurposing is, at the best of times, a challenge. Introducing "generosity" into a church and a city that thinks the whole world owes it something is even more interesting!

As I began to strategise how I would ensure that generosity was a part of the fabric, conversation and activity of BCC, I began to study and think about why people would fight this culture that I would be introducing. I knew that there would be a fight because when I started modelling generosity (by paying the bill every time we took people out, sending scores of texts to people giving encouragement and inviting people round to our home on a daily basis), I began to hear whispers:

"He's a millionaire who's bankrolling the church..."

And,

"It's alright for him in his Audi A4..." (which is highly offensive seeing as it's an Audi A6!)

What I began to discover is that not everyone can be generous. What I began to unveil is that GENEROSITY is intrinsically linked to FREEDOM and I had to bring the revelation of the freedom that was ours before I could facilitate a generous culture in the house.

Many Christians struggle with GENEROSITY because they are not fully embracing the FREEDOM they are called to live in.

Unpacking

Psalm 18:19 clearly tells us that our God delights in us so much that He BRINGS us to a SPACIOUS place. I capitalise these two words intentionally because I want to highlight the reality of our situation. What I now realise is that even though we are brought to and now live *in* a spacious, open, vast, expansive and abundant place, if we don't know it then we won't experience it.

I once lived in a beautiful market town in the Derbyshire Dales. Wirksworth is a small town with a population of approximately 9,000. I was a 12-year old boy when my family moved from Stoke on Trent to Wirksworth. Moving from a city to a market town in the Derbyshire Dales was a difficult move. Leaving behind the friends and comforts of my home city was something I struggled with.

What alleviated the initial difficulty was that we lived in what seemed to be the middle of nowhere. I used to walk into the vast countryside and stand in the middle of fields where there was not a single soul. I remember standing, looking and realising that only God could hear me and as a 12-year old boy with a solid relationship with my God, I shouted as loud as I could to Him, calling on Him regarding my situation.

The freedom of that spacious place facilitated an expressive conversation with God that I could not have had on the city high street.

To establish generosity then, the first step is to equip people with the realisation that they live in a spacious place and that God delights in them.

The second step is to look at Jesus.

Everything about Jesus is associated with freedom. Jesus' earthly ministry was *freedom*. What Jesus achieved for mankind was freedom. Luke's Gospel states that Jesus stood in an assembly of people and declared,

"The Spirit of the Lord is upon me, for he has anointed me to bring Good News to the poor. He has sent me to proclaim that captives will be released, that blind eyes will see, that the oppressed will be set free, and that the time of the Lord's favour has come." (Luke 4:18-20)

What's more, Jesus didn't leave anything to presumption. He rolled up the scroll and then audaciously declared,

"The scripture you've just heard has been fulfilled this day."

This message of freedom that Jesus was sent to declare and accomplish was embraced and owned by Jesus Himself.

There is no denying that Jesus is all about FREEDOM. He achieved FREEDOM by GIVING His all. One of the most powerful and emotive verses in the whole canon of Scripture says,

"There is no greater love than to lay one's life down for one's friends." (John 15:13)

Galatians attempts to cement this revelation deep within the very seat of who we are when it says,

"So Christ has truly set us free. Now make sure that you stay free and don't get tied up again." (Galatians 5:1)

Many a Christian, even though they recognise the work of their Saviour, because of a lack of understanding will fail to live in the absolute freedom that Christ has given. They stand in the field of life with no restrictions and merely whisper when they could shout. Many Christians live their life like the mere hint of an expression, when they could be making a bold, eccentric declaration to the world around them.

We are FREE!

Once this paradigm is established the conversation regarding GENEROUS can take place.

FREEDOM for Who?

That same chapter of Galatians pulls this whole conversation together in one profound statement that blows consumerist Christianity out of the water.

Because that is what we face when repurposing church, right?

Self.

It takes time, but when a church realises that it doesn't exist for itself, things can begin to move. When we realise that we are free for others, then GENEROUS begins to become our culture:

"For you have been called to live in freedom, my brothers and sisters. But don't use your freedom to satisfy your sinful nature. Instead, use your FREEDOM to SERVE ONE ANOTHER." (Galatians 5:13)

BOOM!

FREEDOM is intrinsically linked to GENEROSITY.

A church will never be GENEROUS if it is not FREE.

A church that understands and lives in the FREEDOM that Christ gives will develop a GENEROUS culture.

The audacious offerings, the eccentric volunteer hours, the relentless serving and the high calibre ministries that are pouring out from this house don't originate as the result of a demand, but from the revelation that we are FREE!

When this conversation is had with people new to BCC, it is amazing to watch as eyes open and lives spring forth, as the whisper turns to a shout and the jig turns into an eccentric bounce.

Once free people begin to live GENEROUS lives, they express it in extraordinary ways and it is especially evident in the areas of:

- Knowledge: People don't judge how good (or not) the church is, but with a sweet spirit they offer their "know how" – Then together we excel!
- Finance: People don't need to be coerced into giving, but are lavish and eccentric – Then together we resource!
- Corporate Praise: People don't need winding up on a Sunday morning, they are FREE and expressive – Then together we shout praise!
- Relationships: People don't drain each other and our pastors with immature activity – Then together we grow!

There is a spacious place God brings us to where we can be ourselves fully. Then we are truly "blessed to be a blessing".

CULTURAL PILLARS: HONOUR

Written by Paul Jukes, Executive Pastor and Primary Leader

Over the last three and a half years I have had the privilege of being able to talk on the subject of Honour as part of BCC's Connect course. I have tried to put across what the Bible says about it, but I have also tried, and am still learning, to live a life that honours God, my wife and family, my church leaders and those around me. These are some of my discoveries and thoughts along the way.

Today "honour" is often seen as a quaint relic from the past – a "rear view mirror" concept. We talk about those who gave their lives for others in the war and we honour their memory. It is right to do so, but at BCC we believe honour is not only for the dead. More importantly, it is for the living.

Honour means "to esteem" or "put your weight behind". The dictionary definition states it is, "the esteem due or paid to worth; high estimation; a testimony of esteem; any expression of respect or of high quality by words or actions".

I believe that honour has power! The power to change a generation!

Scripture clearly tells us that,

"Those who honour me I will honour." (Psalm 8:5)

WOW! We have the awesome privilege of partnering with the Living God who created you and me, the universe and this small, unique planet called Earth, in the process of *honour!*

At BCC, honour is not simply something we believe in as a concept – it is something we are committed to modelling and, more importantly, communicating and imparting to the next generation.

So *who* should we honour and *how* should we go about it?

Honour God

Jesus Himself points to His foremost priority in John 8:49:

"But I honour my father."

This must therefore also be our foremost priority: to honour the Father's will as expressed in His Word.

To honour His Word is to honour God!

Everything we do should be focused on the One who deserves all honour and praise. When we focus on Him and His kingdom then "everything else is added". Jesus said, "If you love me, you'll obey my commands." We are called to a simple obedience, like the faith of the centurion in Matthew 8 who took Jesus at His word. Jesus Himself was amazed at such simplicity of faith.

Honour those in authority in everyday life

"Honour" should sum up how we conduct ourselves in every area of our life and relationships. This holds true whether you are an employer or an employee, whether you are a public servant or pursuing a professional career.

I have worked in various schools and know how difficult it can be for a Head Teacher to enact vision by uniting a team of people to work together if no culture of honour exists. In such a setting, one can often hear the rumbles of division in a group of people even while the vision is being expressed!

Honouring those who have authority over us in everyday life often means responding to them in a way contrary to how most people would respond. I love what 1 Peter 3:9 says:

"Do not repay evil with evil or insult with insult, but with blessing, because to this you were called so that you may inherit a blessing."

Many people will complain bitterly whenever they feel they have been treated unfairly or have been hurt. While this is a natural reaction, God calls us to a higher way: *to be a blessing to others even when we have been mistreated!* Retaining our honour in the face of opposition or unfair treatment expresses the truth that we trust God to make things right in His time and in His way. We resist the temptation to become judge, jury and executioner over those who hurt us and instead continue to be a blessing, leaving the matter in God's hands.

Honour church leaders

The issue of honouring those whom God has appointed to lead us is a hugely important one. It is tempting to look at our leaders and think, "It's easy for them!" forgetting the enormous personal cost attached to leading God's people. I am very aware of the difficulties and challenges Pastors James and Becky have been through in order to get BCC to where it is. I caught a sense of how difficult their journey had been when I first met them and immediately I felt honoured to be a part of their lives.

When we first taught honour as part of the Cultural Revolution at BCC, we decided to honour the previous leaders. We bought them gifts and celebrated their journey and we also celebrated those who had been in the church for over 20 years. We finished with the well known phrase: "Hats off to the past, coats off to the future!"

Leadership is important in the house, but we also encourage good *FOLLOW-SHIP*:

Put simply, we turn up, support ministries and we learn to serve! What we say we're going to do, we DO!

Honour each other

I love God's house, His body on earth moving together as one, supporting one another, spurring one another on to do greater exploits for His kingdom! At BCC we've seen hundreds of people unite in a vision and then learn to do life together. A culture of honour has made this possible, resonating with the words of Paul:

"Let us esteem each other better than himself. Let each of you look out not only for his own interests, but also for the interests of others." (Philippians 2:3-4)

I love the fact that Paul tells us to love *ourselves* and to love *others*. We mustn't forget that we are God's creation and that He gave us His stamp of approval, saying we were "very good". But we remember that,

"We will not compare ourselves with each other as if one were better and another worse. We have far more interesting things to do with our lives. Each of us is an original." (Galatians 5:26 MSG)

Various practical points have helped us to model honour to the house.

One of the first things I noticed about Pastors James and Becky was how well behaved their boys were and the respect these boys had for their parents. It stood out clearly in a church where previously children were allowed to roam freely, wildly and sometimes ... well, you get the picture! I learnt quickly to model that behaviour and it affected how I looked after my own children.

The way people are introduced when they visit BCC speaks of honour. Visitors are given a huge cheer and everyone stands to their feet. Some even stand on their chairs. When visitors speak to us, everyone listens intently and engages with what they are saying. We are committed to celebrating people!

Having a standard of excellence is something that Pastor James brought into BCC. Now, when I look at a finished job, I ask myself whether it reflects his high standards. Is it BCC? Everything that is BCC is Pastor James and everything that is Pastor James is BCC. I believe that when we look after the "head" then the blessing pours down onto the body (Psalm 133). Honour God, honour those in authority over you in everyday life, honour your church leaders and honour the body of Christ and you will see your own life transformed.

CULTURAL PILLARS: POSITIVE

You've got to admit that when we look at the Church in our nation – when I look at the Christians in my city, the church that I inherited, and even when I look at myself – we rarely use our brainpower!

It's almost taken as read that when we get saved we should leave the God-given brain we possess (however intelligent we are) at the door of the church building because we are now "Spirit led".

Almost like we lose our minds!

Yet the reverse happens in Scripture.

Let's take Moses for example. When he has an encounter with God, we see his academic prowess isn't too hot when he delivers one of Scripture's most defining and revealing answers to the question, "What do you have in your hand?" His answer? "A stick!" Yet, we see this guy demonstrate the most excellent example of leadership in bringing a people out of slavery.

How about Gideon, who showed great cowardice (Judges 6 and 7) in his initial encounter with God and then reveals immense bravery in attacking the enemy? Or take David, described as "the runt" of the family (see 1 Samuel 16:11 MSG), who receives a mandate from God and then takes down a giant in front of his family! There are so many examples in Scripture that lead us to believe that when we encounter God *then* the brain we have, the gifting that is God-given and the character we *really* possess comes to the surface.

When we encounter God we really begin living the adventure that He intended and designed us to live.

What I wanted to do was equip the people, the church, with a highly explosive stick of dynamite that would empower them to think differently.

I wanted to give them Scripture that they could pull to the surface every time they needed to challenge a wrong way of thinking regarding themselves, others, our church and our city!

The premise for this was: if I could get us to *think* differently, then we would *behave* differently. Or, as Romans 12:2 states, we would be *"transformed by the renewing of our minds."*

The scripture, that stick of dynamite we use, is 1 Corinthians 2:16:

"WE HAVE the MIND of CHRIST."

Let's break that down.

WE: This means ALL of us who belong to Christ. If you're saved, then Paul is talking to you as well as the church in Corinth.

HAVE: This is a present tense declaration. Not past, not future, but present tense.

The MIND of CHRIST: This simply means we have Jesus' mind on things. We think about them like He does.

So to me, it's simple.

We, as HIS church should think like HE thinks. Our thoughts should align themselves with HIS thoughts. If our thinking doesn't fit how HE thinks, then we are the ones with the problem. It is WE who are wrong, not the MIND of CHRIST.

Right?

Right!

So then I unpacked some of the thinking that gripped the church and began to check whether it aligned itself to the WORD made flesh.

To begin this process of causing our thinking to be POSITIVE and biblical let's start with a subject at random, such as...

...YOU! (It wasn't that random!)

The way many of us think about ourselves is firstly not biblical and secondly not beneficial. If we can develop the MIND of CHRIST regarding who we are personally, then corporately we can be the AWESOME place that God intends. This is a painful process, but it is good and has sensational effects.

Understand that you and I were formed before we existed. Understand that we were more than formed, we were handcrafted (Genesis 2:7, Psalm 119:73). It gets better when we realise that we are "known" by Him. I love this. When anyone goes to a party or a function and the host shouts across the crowd, "Hey! Come on in!" it elevates our posture and empowers us because we are "known". The King "knows" us and shouts over the crowd, "Hey! Come on in!" (Jeremiah 1:5).

I desperately want people to know that our God delights in us (Psalm 18:19), even when we sometimes fail to delight in ourselves. The God of the whole universe delights in us SO much that HE brings us into a spacious place. Life isn't meant to be tight and demanding. Yes, there are seasons, but we are called to live in the SPACIOUS place that HE brings us to, simply because HE DELIGHTS in us.

There will always be the person who will say, "Now come on, don't get carried away, I'm only human."

No you're not!

You are one who has found grace in the eyes of the Lord! You have been forgiven!

You are a generation-transforming, devil-bashing, world-conquering Jesus freak! You are a Holy Spirit filled, miracle-working, city-shaking, God-designed, God-alive, loved and cherished child of the KING!

Now, if every Christian believed that about themselves then I'm reckoning church would be that AWESOME place that Jacob discovered. Think about it, Jesus clearly stated, *"Love your neighbour as you love yourself"* (Matthew 22:39). If we fail to rightly esteem ourselves, then what are we going to think of our neighbours? I encourage all of us to stop beating on ourselves and start to love on ourselves a little more. We'll be far more effective in loving our communities!

Corporately, we have to start thinking about the Church as Christ thinks about the Church. Church is the ONLY thing Jesus is going to build and HE describes it as UNSTOPPABLE! Matthew 16:18 shows that Jesus publicly declares that HIS Church is to be *"so expansive with energy that not even the gates of hell can stop it."* (MSG)

As I first preached "Positive", I began seeing that glisten of life again in the eyes of BCCers; that belief in themselves; that confidence to do great exploits and that zest for Jesus! Yes, there was passion stirring, but it was a POSTIVE mindset that was beginning to occur. A paradigm shift was empowering individuals and BCC as a whole.

Thus, people's outlook on our city radically changed. The idea of waiting and crying, "Revive us Lord!" went and the download of revelation came: *"The whole city celebrates when the godly succeed"* (Proverbs 11:10). It provided the aspiration for the church to arise and stop pecking around in the dirt. It was great to watch as a whole church began to realise it was called to be a "Royal Priesthood" (see 1 Peter 2:9), a mighty army, an unstoppable force and the outworking of Jesus' love for this city.

The mobilisation of a church, at this point, had commenced!

SELAH...

Now remembering that culture is established by default or by design, it is imperative to continuously assess the building and development of the desired, designed culture. One of the main difficulties I discovered in communicating culture is that while people listened to the preach or communication about the desired, designed culture, they filtered this and "heard" it from their perspective, gained from another organisation's default culture.

Culture is more than a preaching series. It is more than an academic conversation. It is more than simply knowing.

It has to be cultivated.

That means creating a catalyst to see and prove the *outworking* of the designed culture. For instance, it is easy to talk about *generosity*, even for someone who is not generous. However, when the challenge comes to be generous and there is no hiding place, then the correct assessment can be made as to whether an organisation *is* generous or not. Establishing the desired, designed culture will bring confrontation, so it is essential for the leader, his team and those who have decided to embrace this new culture to ensure that they cultivate the designed and refuse to capitulate to the default.

It is imperative that communication of the desired, designed culture moves to reality. Lose the power struggle here and the default setting, with its long term strength, will revert and abort, stifle and kill any new cultivation taking place.

A BCC STORY: DAVE & FAITH

My family and I joined BCC after realising that we needed more from local church. We needed to be stretched and we needed to grow. We had some friends who already went to BCC and, from our very first visit, we sensed that this was a house that had excellent leadership and character.

We have two sons who both go to City Youth, which is awesome. They are being encouraged to be all that they can be. We have had the privilege of seeing our sons growing in Christ, being happy to come to the house and encouraged to study for themselves and share what they find.

BCC is a church where you are inspired to be all that you can be. What no one tells you though, is that the knock-on effect is you are challenged and challenged some more because growing means you have to change. It's not easy, but it's worth it and we wouldn't have it any other way.

The journey we have been on since coming to BCC has been nothing but exciting, positive and life changing, both for our sons and us. We are privileged to call ourselves BCCers.

A BCC STORY: WAYNE & JULIE

30th September 2007. This was the start of our journey with what
would become Breathe City Church. Wayne was not yet
a Christian. I had been saved since 1994.
I had two dreams: to see my husband fall in love with
Jesus and to work for my church.

30th September 2007 was the day that my daughters
and I came along to see what was happening at BCC.
What we experienced that day led us all make a decision to
call this church our home. The teaching, preaching, worship
and friendliness all blew our minds.
It was what we had dreamed of.

My husband, Wayne, came along to an event on
8th August 2008. Andy Hawthorne came to preach and
gave the call for salvation. One of my dreams became a
reality that night. Wayne is now the ministry director for
the ministry that ran the event where he gave his life to Jesus!

As I write these words my position at BCC is Office Manager.
Yes, dream number two has also become a reality!

Breathe City Church is awesome. Jesus is building His Church.
People who join us and rise to the challenge, grow and flourish.

And this is just the beginning...

CULTURAL PILLARS: HEALTH

Allow me be so bold as to say that I genuinely believe one of the primary faults of my generation is that we are fixated on the subject of church growth.

We have some sensational leaders in the field of church growth and I wholeheartedly endorse anyone working towards church growth. If we are honest, though, anyone with any leadership gift can gather a crowd. That is *not* what God told me to do. God instructed me to *build* a church!

Big difference!

Becky and I are immensely privileged to be the parents of two sensational young boys, and for who we believe God has a wondrous future in store! Becky is a brilliant mum and my hat goes off to all mums out there – you do such an incredible job!

As brilliant a mum as Becky is, I have never once heard her cry for help in regard to making our boys bigger. Never, in all of the eight years we have been parents, have we ever grabbed our boys' arms and legs and attempted to stretch them to ensure that they become bigger than they are now.

No. That would be insane!

Any understanding parent knows that one creates a healthy environment for a child to reside in and naturally the child will grow. It would be absurd for a parent to enforce growth upon a young body. All responsible parents know that dietary, environmental, relational, spiritual, educational, moral and psychological development are essential for a child's growth – not external force.

So why on earth do we do it to church?

Seriously, we need to get a grip and realise that we are insane if we think we can "force" church growth to occur. It's ludicrous to manufacture church growth. It's absurd to blame man-made effort for a supernatural phenomenon. Jesus builds HIS Church! Nothing more, nothing less!

Some of the farcical stuff that has been said about churches that grow fast, including BCC, is absolutely ridiculous! People must be out of their minds to say such crazy things like "hype … sheep stealing … manipulation" and other nonsensical stuff!

A young child grows naturally if they are HEALTHY. Simple. A church grows because it's HEALTHY.

All healthy things grow!

Healthy. What does that mean in regard to church? To me, the easiest way of understanding this is found in Matthew 16:18 where Jesus simply states:

"I will build MY church."

To me it is that simple and we, the church or leaders, have made it so complicated. I believe that a healthy church is one where JESUS is absolutely central. As in the "chief cornerstone" (see Matthew 21:42). As in not the constitution, the political persuasion, the loudest voice, the biggest giver or the best preferred style – but JESUS.

JESUS.

To me Mark 2:1-12 gives us a great illustration of what a "house" looks like when JESUS is central to everything that is happening. You'll know the passage well. It is where four friends bring a crippled friend on a stretcher to Jesus. The house is so packed with people that they are not getting in through the front door. What do they do? Go home? Try the house next door that is more welcoming, serves better coffee or has a more palatable sermon and a sleeker media presentation?

NO!

They have to be at the house where Jesus is. They climb up and, at roof level, rip into the limiting restrictions for the whole community to see and lower their friend to the feet of Jesus.

This whole story shows how we should build church, so that Jesus is central to all activity. What do we learn from it?

Firstly, these were friends who were going to the house where they knew Jesus was. This is massive! They were FRIENDS! We have lost the art of "doing life together". Honestly, we must work at our relationships. What is the deal with going next door because we fall out over the smallest thing?

Listen, if we know JESUS is in the house, let's get over our differences and BE FRIENDS. This requires us to BE FRIENDLY! One of the greatest joys I have in watching BCC grow is the quality of the relationships. Psalm 133 says that where people dwell, as in, reside together in UNITY, then HE commands the blessing.

Blessing comes when unity is established.

Secondly, they brought their friend who was a cripple. Because these friends knew that this guy's answer, JESUS, was in the house, they took ownership of BRINGING him. Note that I used the word "brought" not "bought". Too often we bribe people into coming to church on the promise of great coffee, "fresh expressions", a guest speaker or another gimmick that we come up with.

When JESUS is in the house people won't need an excuse to bring their friends – they will know that JESUS is the only headline that is required!

Thirdly, they LIFTED the lid on LIMITING restrictions. I have heard many a preach on this, but it is so true. When JESUS is in the house the "excuse culture" disappears. When a church is void of Jesus' breath we create every excuse as to why it's not happening. We don't need to go into the excuses we manufacture, what we do need to say is that we need HIS presence! Stop with the excuses!

I firmly believe that every church leader and every person genuinely desiring to be a leader should, at least once in their lifetime, do a 40-day fast. It is my conviction that a 40-day fast does many things, including eradicating the excuse culture in church.

Seriously.

You may right now be making excuses as to why you have never done a 40-day fast ... which proves my theory. Leader, if you are serious about lifting the lid on your church then please consider a 40-day fast.

Fourthly, when JESUS is in the house then HEALING and FORGIVE-NESS follow. Over the last two and a half years we have seen people make decisions to follow JESUS every week. We have seen people healed during the praise. We have endless stories of lives trans-formed.

We are surprised, but we shouldn't be. BCC experienced 92 con-secutive weeks where people made decisions for JESUS. I was gun-ning for 100 weeks and during the 93rd week we saw no one make a decision.

I was gutted.

I wondered why and this thought came (was it God's whisper?) "The 93rd week was the abnormal week, not the 92 consecutive weeks." Week 94 saw someone make a decision and we have pretty much carried on seeing people make decisions each week to turn their lives around and begin walking with Jesus.

When JESUS is present, lives are changed.

Fifthly, there was much MOANING and CRITICISM surrounding this event. The truth is, when JESUS is around the Pharisees don't half give it some! Even when JESUS was walking the earth and people witnessed HIM do amazing things, the Pharisees still criticised.

If it happened to JESUS it will happen to us.

The best thing to do with the Pharisees is ignore them! I just wrote around 300 words to give you a clear example from our story of a pharisaic attitude, but I felt the Holy Spirit telling me to press "de-lete", so I did. Ignore them. Press "delete" when you tell *your* story! Don't give them airtime! JESUS gets the word count!

Sixthly, there is a NEW SOUND of PRAISE. When the man is healed and forgiven, the passage tells us that people praised. When JESUS resides, the sound of praise is unquenchable. The sound of BCC is discussed later in this book.

Finally, when JESUS resides there is ALWAYS NEW REVELATION. I love this, the passage tells the reader that people exclaimed,
"We have never seen anything like this before!"

I love that when JESUS resides new "stuff" is happening all the time and there is now no room for the familiar! When JESUS is in the house, be expectant and comfortable with the NEW!

CULTURAL PILLARS: SECURE

I think that one of the most damaging things in church life is *insecurity*. It robs and restricts people from enjoying the Christlike nature that God wants us all to experience.

In order to combat the destructive way in which many people lived, I first had to address this in my own personal life. Secondly, as a church, we walked the journey of discovering that this toxin is everywhere and we have to deal with it if we are to reveal Christ in our city and beyond.

I am amazed at how many of us are like the foolish builder in Matthew 7. We refuse to put into practice what Jesus says and thus live in a diabolical world of insecurity. Like the foolish builder, if we build on the temporal of this world then we will, for sure, not stand the test of time. If we are to build great churches, then we need to build great people with great foundations.

You know about the insecure foundations in today's climate, don't you? The things that are so ridiculous, but upon which people continue to build. Things like other people's opinions, being more attractive than your neighbour, leading a bigger church, becoming more well known, how much of the Bible we know compared to the guy on the row in front, being perceived as "super-spiritual" and all the other really dud stuff that we build on.

Insecurity builds on a whole load of unreliable stuff. It is so dangerous that people who live this way then have to prop themselves up using other people's failings or by clambering through life treading on others.

As a church I knew we had to build in such a way as to love people for who they are and inspire them to become all they can be. Insecure people aren't able to build in this way, so we ourselves had to become secure.

We refused insecurity entry!

"How do we live secure?" was the next, obvious question, because we had generally become so used to living insecure that insecurity seemed "normal" to us. The following is how we got to grips with this.

Firstly, a secure person knows how to stand. As in stand without a prop, without leaning. Isaiah 32:8 says, *"Generous people plan to do what is generous, and they stand firm in their generosity."* As a church we learnt to stand in a place of generosity. We stand when our attention is not on ourselves, but when we are giving ourselves to serve others.

As church, we must learn to stand so that our city can see us.

Secondly, we must understand who we are. Most of our security comes from what we do, but that is temporal. Understanding who we are allows us to be secure. Jesus understood who He was. In Matthew 4 we see Jesus being tempted with the bait of, *"If you are the Son of God…"* and Satan goes on to ask Jesus to "do stuff" to prove who He is – such as telling stones to become bread, jumping off a cliff etc. Jesus didn't respond in the way Satan wanted Him to because Jesus didn't have to. Jesus didn't have to prove who He was. He knew who He was.

What we need to harness in our thinking is that how we conduct ourselves stems from our understanding of who we are. Jesus overcame not by doing but by *being*.

Paul, writing to the church at Ephesus, starts his epistle with three chapters all about *who they are* before talking about what they should be doing. The apostle Paul understood that how a church sees itself determines how it behaves. According to Paul, the church in Ephesus was blessed, chosen, predestined, given, redeemed, forgiven, included, marked, made alive, saved, raised up, seated with Christ, created, brought near, full of fellow citizens and members, a part of things, and built together.

Paul's observation of the church in Ephesus applies also to the Church today. We must start to understand who we are.

Thirdly, secure people *enjoy* being. I knew that the church we were to become, and now can give testimony to, was one that was going to be full of joy and vitality. There is so much misery in the world and the Church should be bringing a smile. There is a sacred cow paradigm that says that everything spiritual in life must be serious. No! It's simply not true! Jesus was anointed with joy above all others (Hebrews 1:9).

We can enjoy being us.

Life is great.

"Trust in the Lord and do good. Then you will live safely in the land and prosper." (Psalm 37:3)

"The lowly will possess the land and will live in peace and prosperity." (Psalm 37:11)

"They will not be disgraced in hard times, even in famine they will have more than enough." (Psalm 37:19)

All these verses lead us to a place where we can enjoy life.

"So I saw that there is nothing better for people than to be happy in their work. That is why we are here! No one will bring us back from death to enjoy life after we die." (Ecclesiastes 3:22)

"And it is a good thing to receive wealth from God and the good health to enjoy it. To enjoy your work and accept your lot in life – this is indeed a gift from God." (Ecclesiastes 5:19)

These biblical truths lead us to believe that we can actually enjoy our work and the money we earn from it. I am convinced that some people suffer in their employment because they feel it makes them "holier", like some kind of perjury. I tell BCCers often, and you the reader, if you don't enjoy your job, CHANGE it! Please don't tell me, "It's not that simple." Yes, it is!

One for the men: Ecclesiastes 9:9 tells us that we can enjoy our wives. We shouldn't be moaning about "her indoors", we should re-alise afresh that she is a gift from God, a princess of the King and we are so privileged that we get to do life with her. ENJOY YOUR WIFE – it's biblical!

There is so much more I could say about this, but the proven sci-entific way of starting the journey towards joy begins by gradually turning the corners of your mouth upwards. That's it!

You're smiling!

Now live that way!

Fourthly, secure people are confident. It is my belief that church has been robbed of its confidence because religion has stipulated that confidence is arrogance. Confidence is a good thing. Confidence is biblical. We can be confident in Christ according to Hebrews 10:19-22:

"And so, dear brothers and sisters, we can boldly enter heaven's Most Holy Place because of the blood of Jesus. By his death, Jesus opened a new and life-giving way through the curtain into the Most Holy Place. And since we have a great High Priest who rules over God's house, let us go right into the presence of God with sincere hearts fully trusting him."

Hebrews 13:6 tells us that we can be confident in our circumstanc-es, whatever they may be:

"So we can say with confidence, 'The Lord is my helper, so I will have no fear. What can mere people do to me?'"

And in reading Philippians 3 it is clear that Paul wants the church at Phillippi, and us, to understand that we can be confident in our call-ing. Our cities and communities are crying out for someone to take the lead. As Church, we should be confident in our calling to be salt and light and a city on a hill (Matthew 5:14).

A secure church can make a huge impact on a city and a community.

CULTURAL PILLARS: TRUE

The final cultural pillar is all about the arrow.

When it comes to understanding how they are put together, arrows are fascinating. They have three components. Firstly, the arrow has a tip. This is the part that causes the penetration. It is the part that carries the weight. The second part is the shaft. The shaft is what causes the arrow to fly straight or "true". The third part, the flight, facilitates the arrow's ability to glide through the air.

When looking at church life we can clearly see that God has anointed or gifted churches. The "tip" of a church that can cause breakthrough or penetration is God-given. We can very often see the "flight" of a church when we look at how the Holy Spirit works in and through church life, giving it the ability to glide through time and difficulty, opposition and adversity.

What we are focusing on here though is the *shaft* of church life.

This could also be identified as the *character* of the church. When Paul addresses the church in Corinth, he clearly recognises the anointing (tip) that the church carries. I can imagine that it had great ministries and sensationally talented people. Paul most definitely acknowledges the work of the Holy Spirit (flight) in the church. Oh my goodness, imagine what the Corinthians were seeing happen to have Paul write to them in such away! Yet Paul, in writing to the church, focuses on addressing the central character and behaviour (shaft) of the church.

Any arrow or church can have a recognised anointing (tip). It can have sensational operation of the Holy Spirit (flight). But if the shaft (character) isn't straight when the archer needs to use the arrow it will never fly "true" and fulfil its destiny or objective. As church we have to deal with the issue of character in order to hit the "bullseye".

We have to be TRUE.

I love how Paul in 2 Corinthians (10:5-6) uses hunting language when he says,

"We destroy every proud obstacle that keeps people from knowing God. We capture their rebellious thoughts and teach them to obey Christ. And after you have become fully obedient, we will punish everyone who remains."

That's powerful phraseology by Paul. I mentioned earlier that a great church doesn't have lumpy carpets. If great church is to be established, there is no sweeping things under the rug, because one day we will trip up on them. We have to deal with the things we have to deal with if we are to be true.

To help with this process we need a commitment to the following:

Firstly, DISCIPLESHIP and DETERMINATION. Character should always be put above charisma in church. I have seen too much "high on style, low on content" type ministry to ignore this. We have to be committed to being disciples of Christ and putting into practice what HE wants in our lives, even when it hurts, if we are to build great church. As an individual I have to be determined in this process. I go to the gym and it hurts. I run six miles, five days a week and it hurts. But I am determined to stick with the discipline because it keeps me on track, keeps me true.

It is the same with church.

Secondly, FOCUS and FOLLOW. Our focus should never be on each other, the leaders, the music or the great events that we put on. Our focus should always be Jesus and the city we are trying to reach. With Jesus and our city as the focus we have a common denominator that keeps us all together. I hate war, but it teaches me that when there is a common purpose, even nations that don't really like each other come together in unity because there is a common denominator. In this, we should work hard at "follow-ship" also. There is much written and talked about regarding leadership, but there are two ingredients to great church: great leadership and great followship.

Training people to follow is really important.

Thirdly, we need commitment to RECOGNISE and not REMAIN. Developing a "green light" policy is so important to any process of repurposing. Jesus clearly said, "Go" (Matthew 28) and therefore we must recognise that there is a mission field to be harvested. It is imperative that we never remain in the same place, but that we are always moving and achieving effectiveness. If I get into a car and the scenery, after several hours into the journey, doesn't change, it means that I am only sat in my car – I'm not going anywhere!

Fourthly, we need a commitment to be REAL and not RELIGIOUS. We will never deal with the elephant in the room, the pressing questions and issues that need to be faced, if we live with a religious spirit and are not real enough to ask, "What's the elephant doing in the room?"

If something is not working then we should ask, "Why?" If fruit is not being seen then we must be real enough to address the issues. Religion puts a mask on every Sunday morning and says, "Everything is okay" when, looking at society, we can see full well that it is not.

If we are to be "true" to the mandate that Jesus gave His Church then we must be real and not religious.

Once a church is committed to the above then progress can be made.

What needs to happen next, if a church is going to hit the bullseye and fulfil its destiny, is that an understanding of the following must be grasped:

We need to fully understand what SUBMISSION and SERVANTHOOD mean. Submission is a word that is very often abused in church, usually by leaders who use it to simply get people to do what they want.

The world has developed negative baggage and connotations regarding submission, but it can be best explained when we look at a "smorgasbord". This European way of dining is something to behold. Every attendee brings a dish and then the feast begins with all involved filling their plates with the vast selection before them. Submission is simply to put my gifts, abilities and even my life on the table. Submission is an offering of one's self. Submission is a beautiful thing and if a church understands it, then the menu of what we can offer to our city is sensational!

Servanthood also carries negative connotations. It is a label that gets placed on what some people consider "menial" tasks. This is so wrong. From what scholars tell me, I understand "to serve" to mean "a stooping down to make it easier for another". As in, "If you drop something, I will bend down and pick it up for you." Imagine that: a church with the understanding that we are called to serve, to stoop down and make it easier for another.

We need to also understand what COVERING and ACCOUNTABILITY mean. At a Jewish wedding, so I'm told, you will usually see a "chuppah". A chuppah is a canopy, about the size of a large beach towel, supported by four poles under which the bride and groom stand during their wedding ceremony. It is symbolic of covering and accountability. The four corners of the material represent the four promises of God to the people of Israel in Exodus 3-6: I will take you out, I will rescue you, I will redeem you, and I will take you to be with me.

These four great promises demonstrate the covering of God linked with the Shekinah glory in 1 Kings 8:10-11. These four promises are outworked as: ownership, protection, redemption and provision. This is such a beautiful picture of what covering and accountability should mean and represent in church life.

And, finally, we need to develop an understanding of LEADERSHIP and LONGEVITY. The front of a ship is the part that causes its penetration through the waves. If we are to be true and fulfil our destiny or hit our bullseye, then we need to champion leadership and do the best we can to help and support them as they breakthrough for the rest of the ship to follow with ease.

Leadership needs to be focused on breaking through whilst the rest of the ship needs to ensure that it keeps up with the progress that is being made. Church isn't a club we come to, but a journey with a mission. There is reason to it. This journey is going to take a lifetime. It has longevity to it, which means we can build our lives around this mission to reach our city. The phrase "doing life together" takes on a greater importance when we understand that there is an air of destiny about this journey that we are on together.

OBSERVATIONS OF CHANGE

In establishing culture there must be an absolute understanding that, in effect, the previously established culture has to be eradicated. It must also be understood that buildings, media, music, visuals and distribution material all convey the message of the culture, but it is people who carry and care for the culture.

This is why we can watch many a promo and look at lots of websites that seem outstanding and convey a culture of excellence, but when seen in real life the "product" can often be quite disappointing. Holidays are prepared for months in advance, paid for and booked on the evidence of the catalogue. Yet how many horror stories do we hear of people who arrive at their dream holiday to find partially built hotels and rat infested restaurants?

It's the same in church.

We can *portray* desired culture through media, websites and other paraphernalia, but it is the people that matter. People carry and care for the culture.

Leaders cultivate culture.

It is imperative, therefore, that leaders not only constantly communicate the culture through everything that is said, produced or presented, but also *live* the culture. In communicating the responses to our cultural revolution, the first thing to say is that myself, Becky and the other leaders of BCC had to begin to address the areas of our lives that were not demonstrating the culture of BCC.

Leadership is visible. If the leader is not exuberant in corporate praise, the people won't be. If the leader is not passionate about reading Scripture, the people won't be. If the leader is not generous, then the people won't be.

John Maxwell was so correct when he coined the phrase, "It all rises and falls on leadership."

The second thing to recognise is that culture has to be "caught, taught or sort". I used this phrase a lot when I first arrived in Stoke on Trent.

Caught

This describes the person who gets it straight away. This type of person is a dream. It's a heart thing. This type of person simply catches the culture. They realise we aren't simply preaching fancy messages on Clean, Generous, Honour, Positive, Health, Secure and True. This type of person understands that this is who we are, this is our culture and they embrace it, even change to become a living stone in the house.

This type of person will make the journey of transition. Be warned: this type of person is the minority.

Taught

The second type of person has to be "taught". I prefer to believe that people are fantastic. I choose to trust people. I believe in people. I love people. So when a person carries a different culture to that of the house, I choose to believe that it is not a "heart" issue but a "head" issue.

It is not a change of heart that is required, but simply a change in thinking.

A change in thinking is not going to happen as quickly as it will for the person who *catches* the culture. They need more time for the penny to drop. They are good people, but they need more communication, more examples and more space to realise that change is happening and they have a choice as to whether they want to adopt the new culture or reject the change.

What we have to ensure is that change is happening either way.

Sort

The third type of person is "sort". This is more difficult.

I have no problem in confronting someone who is rebellious, divisive, disruptive or even demonic. I have no issue with fronting up to a bully, a bragger or even an abusive character. But I do struggle to have the conversation where, actually, a person is simply not getting the culture of the house and it has to be challenged directly.

I struggle because, in the cold light of day, does it really matter that this person is negative rather than positive or perhaps not so generous as they could be?

Actually, in regard to building great church and a kingdom culture, yes, it does matter!

A person's behaviour may have been deemed "normal" or "acceptable" before, but during and after change they stick out like a sore thumb.

For the sake of the whole, the individual has to be challenged to shape up.

It needs *sorting*.

Sometimes in this scenario the leader will be called a control freak for challenging counter-cultural attitudes. Or a dictator, a bully, or an enforcer. Phrases like "You don't love me" or "This is a cult" will be used.

These and similar phrases all mean the same thing: "I'm not in control any more. I don't like it and I don't want to change."

The process of change would be a dream if everyone "caught" the culture.

It would be a great process if it could be "taught" to everyone in the church. But the reality is that conflict will come as, in certain cases, the leader has to "sort" the contrasting attitudes. The reality is that when bringing change in church life people will leave because they are not prepared to adopt the new culture.

Running the "Connect" course three times a year really helps BCC to ensure that new people grasp hold of our culture. Occasionally we will ask people to do "Connect" again as we can see that they aren't carrying or caring for the culture of BCC.

We have noted that every organisation, institution and even church has a culture, by design or by default.

When it is by design, "Caught, Taught or Sort" is essential.

A BCC STORY: MIKE & JANET

When it was announced that Pastors James and Becky were
coming as leaders of what was The Bethel, we began to dare to
hope that church could start to become all that we had hoped,
dreamed and prayed it would be.

Then came the reality of facing the changes that needed
to come, the price that had to be paid: getting to know and
choosing to trust a leader again and facing our own fears,
hurts and disappointments of the past.
It is only changed people who can really bring about change.
There have been many times when we have said,
"We don't think we can do this."
Facing the daily challenge of doing new things
or old things in a new way is stretching.

Many of the things that Pastor James introduced in the
first few weeks really resonated with us and helped and
confirmed to us that this was God at work again. Along with this
came sadness as some people struggled to adapt
to the changes that were coming thick and fast.
It is always sad when people you felt were a part of your
house and family suddenly feel the need to separate,
divorce and cut themselves off from you.
But we have realised that what we are looking for
is people to "do life" with, not just people who are in
the same programme or meeting.

It is very exciting to be amongst quality people.
To see their commitment and heart for the house is inspiring.
As we see people growing in their faith there are
few words to express how thrilling this is.
It is humbling to see God at work.

We have been on a journey through good times and hard times.
We have learnt and continually learn the following two things:

Church is not about me.
Culture is massively important.

These last few years have been the most exciting and
we look forward to even better and greater times.

PART
3
THERE
IS
ALWAYS
A
COST

Every church that
needs repurposing
also has strong and
controlling elements
that need to be
challenged

INTRODUCTION

The last three and a half years have been sensational.

It has been such a privilege to watch, observe, participate and experience the building that takes place when Jesus graces a church with a season such as we have experienced. I have many friends across the planet who heap encouragement and adulation on the God-phenomenon that has happened here at Breathe City Church.

It truly has been amazing. This section of the book, however, tells the story from a different perspective.

Change is not easy.

There is always a cost.

This chapter of the book is designed to highlight some of the difficulties experienced when bringing change. If this book is encouraging change, then it should also highlight the cost.

There is always a cost.

Before embarking on the journey of repurposing church it would be beneficial to understand some of the dimensions, strategies and weapons that are used to abort, stifle and divert what needs to occur.

This section of the book may highlight why church rarely repurposes.

Some of the experiences recounted in this chapter are X-rated and shocking. However, to avoid making the reader aware of the difficulties involved in change would be unwise.

There is always a cost!

JEZEBEL AND AHAB

It is my firm opinion that every church that needs repurposing also has strong and controlling elements that need to be challenged. I am not necessarily talking about personalities. I am most definitely talking about controlling spirits that manifest themselves through people and mindsets.

I have already stated that it is essential, before any repurposing occurs, that a FOD walk be undertaken and understanding of the history appreciated.

The church we inherited had a very public history with some great leaders, such as Pastor Peter Johnson, who did an immense work that I personally believe this "now" generation is benefiting from.

The church we inherited also had a very negative history of good men, full of integrity and godly character, having to capitulate to the Jezebel spirit. Leaders were never fully leading the church because of the control of this spiritual phenomenon. Many have written or spoken about this, but few have modelled an example of how to deal with it.

Initially, it was evident that the Jezebel spirit was manifesting itself through a small group of women who were involved in various teams throughout the church. In effect, the Jezebel spirit was controlling every aspect of the church. As we know from Scripture (1 Kings 19 and 21), the Jezebel spirit creates fear in the office of the Prophet and stirs up lies and dissension with the leaders or fathers of the city. Both tactics cause a man to be disempowered. In Elijah's case he demonstrated fear and came to the conclusion that he wanted to die:

"I have had enough, Lord ... Take my life for I am no better than my ancestors who have already died." (1 Kings 9:4)

The other tactic that the spirit of Jezebel uses is a letter writing exercise that I am sure, had the technology been available in 1 Kings 21, would have occurred via Facebook and email. Jezebel spurts playground lies that feed on the insecurity and fear of leaders in a city. False accusations against good men like Naboth, using super-spiritual tones, resulted in the public execution of a good man:

"In her letters she commanded, 'Call the citizens together for fasting and praying, and give Naboth a place of honour. And then seat two scoundrels across from him who will accuse him of cursing God and the king. Then take him out and stone him.'" (1 Kings 21:9-10)

The first "layer" of the Jezebel spirit left the church pretty much immediately. Personally, it caused me to celebrate because I thought that this confrontation was easier than I expected. However, what I went on to learn, I now desperately want other leaders to observe and take note of. Within twelve months, a known character came to BCC, not knowing that a new regime was being established. The then leaders panicked because they knew that in the past this person's behaviour had been very destructive.

The leadership team at that time literally begged for an entrance course to be established to ensure that the said person and their accomplices knew that this was a different church. "Connect" was created to communicate much of what you have already read, with the participants spending ten sessions with me personally. This course has actually become the bedrock of BCC and is a great resource for other church leaders desiring to repurpose church for the next generation.

So what lessons did I learn?

Firstly that it is pointless confronting the person or personality. A leader must confront, speak to and challenge the *spirit of Jezebel*.

Unless a person recognises that they are being used in this way, they will not change. Jezebel is poison. It spreads. In situations where emotions are high and times are traumatic the Jezebel spirit uses such opportunities to get people "on side". A leader must understand that this is a spiritual matter. People will make decisions and walk paths for which they will have to face the consequences in the future. This is not the leader's responsibility. The leader must focus on removing the spirit of Jezebel from the house!

Don't listen to the lies. Refuse to live in fear. Ensure that an undivided team is not penetrated. Pray and fast in order to strengthen anointing. Preach the sermons that need to be preached whilst dealing in grace with people.

The second lesson is one I definitely wish I knew beforehand, because then the stuff we went through would not have occurred. Jezebel only resides in a house where Ahab resides. If the Ahab spirit is removed then Jezebel has no legal right to be there and operate. What characterises the spirit of Ahab? Petulant, pathetic, sulky, attention-seeking behaviour. But when this is ignored, it leaves. When it knows it isn't going to get its "vineyard" or its own way, then it leaves in a selfish tantrum. Let it leave.

Don't chase the person either. A great inspiration to me in this regard is Pastor Dave Gilpin of Hope City Church, Sheffield. He once gave me a sensational piece of advice regarding the situation of the "Ahab" leaving:

"If the horse has bolted from the stable, never run after it."

This is so true. Many a leader will chase after people and try to persuade "Ahabs" to stay.

But, unintentionally, the leader (usually one who is more pastoral) will pander to the sulky behaviour of the spirit of Ahab and thus keep this spirit in the house, thus giving Jezebel the legal right to reside also.

Here are some quotes from Facebook and emails I have received to show how Jezebel and Ahab manipulate the truth and attempt to create fear in a leader with playground tactics, spreading malicious rumours:

"It's funny how people change things to suit themselves..."

"You have failed before you have even started..."

"The BCC Church is man-driven, not God-driven..."

"Looks money-driven..."

"This place is a cult..."

"Witchcraft..."

"It's shady, it's two-faced..."

"Bully..."

"Law, cultish behaviour..."

"You don't deserve the title 'Pastor'..."

"I do have a lot of reservations about the style of ministry and I would advise you not to go there ... It's not a good move in my opinion..."

And here are a few practical tactics that I put in place to ensure that such confrontation was managed with victory as the outcome. I use the word "victory" intentionally, because this conflict is a battle for the leadership of the house. A leader must win!

Don't believe the "everybody is saying" tactic. It is a falsehood. Jezebel and Ahab work through gossip, corrupt speech and play on people's insecurities. Their accusations are false and they are not as powerful as they want people to believe. It's like the scripture that tells us Satan roams around "like" a roaring lion (1 Peter 5:8). "Like" tries to get us to believe something that is not the case.

Leader: you have the mandate to lead. Refuse to be manipulated by listening to or reasoning with either the spirit of Ahab or Jezebel. They will get into your thinking and confuse your self-belief. YOU are called of God to lead – do so. If everyone leaves, so be it, but you must not capitulate! (Everyone will not leave, that is simply what Jezebel and Ahab want you to think).

Pay no attention to the church leaders who the Jezebel and Ahab spirit run to. If a leader is naïve enough to run after and invite Jezebel and Ahab into his church, then fine. It simply means that they are not in yours. What will happen is Jezebel and Ahab will set up shop in that church and quality people will leave there and come to you. It's a win-win situation.

Speak truth. Very often leaders are careful about their wording. Don't be. Be accurate. Leave no doubt in people's minds what you are saying. Jezebel and Ahab twist truth and hide their manipulation with lies. Make sure you deal in the currency of truth. Don't hint. Don't be polite. Be very definitive and poignant with your words and actions.

Give Jezebel and Ahab no room for manoeuvre. Naboth and Elijah are crippled. 2 Kings 9 reveals that a Jehu spirit or mindset is what is required to defeat this opposition. Pastoral counselling won't work here. It needs the Jehu in the leader to rise up and "go after" the conflict. Have the conversations, arrange the face to face meetings, and stand your ground no matter the cost. If a leader fails to do this then Jezebel and Ahab win!

Jehu states, "What do you know about peace? Fall in behind." Jezebel and Ahab will use "unity", "peace" and other super-spiritual babble to try to get a leader to stand down. DON'T! Create order. People will either fall in line or leave. Either way, the man of God has to establish order in the house.

Once the spirit of Ahab is removed from office it leaves, as pride is always a contributing factor behind it. Once Ahab leaves, Jezebel follows as she has no legal right to be there.

It was at this time of vacation that we really saw the blessing and favour of God descend and we have never looked back! It was BCC's defining moment and a great season of breakthrough.

POVERTY MINDSET AND ACCLIMATISATION

I am a "Stokie".

This city is my home city.

Born at the North Staffs Hospital, season ticket holder and lifelong fan of Stoke City FC and I've bragged throughout my entire existence that I'm from Stoke.

However, during my teens I lived in Derbyshire. I studied in the great city of Nottingham. I then spent 13 years, all of my adult life, in Cardiff, the sensational capital city of Wales.

I am a "Stokie" by birth and by right, but I have a very different mindset.

One year into the journey of repurposing, my now Executive Pastor, Paul Jukes, went to have coffee with a local church leader to engage in conversation since we were planting a congregation in his parish. Paul returned from the meeting, told me of his experience and began downloading the details of the conversation.

Apparently, I was violently criticised in the meeting. This leader especially held the opinion, and I quote,

"He needs to understand the culture of the city in which he is working and building church. He's wrong and it won't last."

Matthew 21:12-17 gives a graphic illustration of what Jesus thought of the culture of a community. He aggressively and passionately "drove" the resident culture out of the temple. Pastor Alan Hewitt

(Newtown) preaches a great sermon regarding Jesus' attitude in ensuring that the house of God has kingdom culture. In repurposing church, one must never capitulate to the resident culture of the church, community or city. Kingdom culture should be established. We are, as church, designed to be counter-cultural.

BCC partners closely with Compassion, a phenomenal international charity that uses child sponsorship as a vehicle to not only help a child and a family out of poverty, but also to communicate the unconditional love of Jesus to parts of the world perhaps forgotten. As part of our partnership BCC works very closely with Lwantama Evangelical Church in Uganda. Recently, Paul and I had the immense privilege of taking a three-day trip to visit and minister in the church. As I was preaching, the greatest thing occurred to me: the church was just like BCC. Different, but the same! Whenever you visit a Jesus-centred church it is always the same, anywhere in the world.

It's called Kingdom Culture.

In repurposing church, a leader absolutely must not give way to the culture of the people, because the leader is working to establish a culture that is based on Scripture, not the resident or historical culture. In today's climate much is written regarding "Missional Church", "Missiology" and "Engaging with Community" – much of which I wholeheartedly agree with. BCC, at present, has 26 ministries and works across 10 diverse sites in our region. We understand "missional" ministry, but we must never lose sight of who we are.

Church should look very different to our communities and cities.

In Matthew 5 Jesus gives us a clear instruction to be counter-cultural. He instructs us to be salt and light, a city on a hill. A great hero, inspiration and mentor of mine, Mal Fletcher, talks powerfully from this passage in Matthew 5 regarding the Church being a city on a hill, being the very micro view of what the macro view of a city should look like. The Church isn't to follow the city's leading. The Church is given of God and is being built by Jesus to draw on the flavour of a city, to preserve the health of a city, to be a light in a city, to bring revelation to a city, to stand out, ahead and above a city. The Church is designed to be a beacon in the community.

What I must do, as a leader, is discover the cultural giants of the area to which I am called. If that giant is damaging the wellbeing of a city, then I should build in direct opposition to that culture and demonstrate something powerful to the community. For instance, Stoke on Trent, in my opinion has an extreme victim and poverty mindset. It really struggles with success and anything new is criticised immediately. In some cases, "new" is simply foreign.

Therefore, the cultural pillars of *Positive* and *Generous* are absolutely fundamental to who we are as a church. We model what it is to have a victor's mindset and we champion successful activity in our city. We work tirelessly at being as generous as we possibly can. All our ministries work towards being self-financing. We don't provide free tea and coffee at BCC, people pay. If a person literally has not got the money to pay for their coffee, a BCCer in the queue will buy them one. The current economic climate and lack of development in our city is epic and yet our financial growth is unbelievable and we are sat on a multi-million pound asset.

Why?

Because we have a kingdom mindset and a kingdom economy. The city isn't dictating our culture, it is the other way around.

We have made a commitment to work very hard and strategically on our offerings. We have had some huge offerings. At the time of writing we are gearing up for our 2011 First Fruits offering where we are unashamedly aiming for £100,000! These offerings are everything about the size, value and numbers and yes, we do talk about it a lot.

But at the same time, I am genuinely not interested in the money. For the first several months at BCC I wasn't even paid. Money doesn't interest me. But the statement that giving makes, does! Every time we take one of these huge offerings we regard it as a prophetic slap in the face of the giant called "Poverty" that has kept this city down for far too long.

I have had Facebook updates written about me by Christians – about the car I drive, about how, to be a member of BCC, you have to submit your bank details so that the church can take your money, about how I am a secret millionaire who is bankrolling the church (I wish that were true!), or about how I have bankrupted the church with mega mortgages and many more. Again, what these people say really doesn't interest me, as I know that we are giving for those who are not yet saved.

The real problem with "Fresh Expressions" and "21st Century Church" is that church has reached a desperate state when we chase after being relevant to a city.

Being "relevant" is not biblical.

Genesis 7:11 tells us that Noah only became relevant when the rain started to pour. If Noah had been "21st Century" and chased relevancy, the ark would never have been built.

It is clear to me that in repurposing church, it is not the relevance to a generation or community that is required, it is the design and blueprint from God that is required. Our "ark" should demonstrate kingdom design.

Church should never chase relevance or be "in keeping" with its community or city. Church should be in front. Church should be established in such a way that when the storms and floods of life occur, the city knows that we are prepared – knows where we are and that the door is open for them to find refuge. That is why BCC is not a church that has mostly transitional growth. It is uncomfortable for consumerist Christians.

The ark no doubt contained an immense amount of excrement from the animals. The ark wasn't a cruise liner one could board with a £4,000 ticket! It was a facility designed to rise above the storm and bring a generation to safe passage. It was an "all hands on deck" type boat. Christians who want to remain "Stokie" in mindset and behaviour have a very short residency at BCC, due to the fact that we don't live that way and we work hard at ensuring our culture stays kingdom.

I'm afraid that the local church leader who Paul met that day was wrong. I do understand the culture of my city, but I refuse to go along with it. I will not allow it to invade the culture of our church. I will continue to ensure that our church is counter-cultural, true to its God-design, and brings a challenge to any cultural giant in the city that is bringing a negative influence.

Leader: never acclimatise to your surroundings. Build church as a city on a hill. Build on a Whole 'Nutha Level and build knowing that kingdom culture will always be counter cultural.

Be the difference by being different.

JOSEPH'S BROTHERS

Joseph is one of my favourite characters in the Bible. His story is a sensational tale of how God works behind the scenes in a person's life and they don't even realise. Joseph's example is a great encouragement to us and helps us understand that the scenario we face is not the issue, but our heart response and activity is. Joseph is a great example that integrity is always the defining factor, whether you are in prison or occupying the office of Prime Minister.

Years ago a pastor gave me a book, *God Meant it for Good* by R.T. Kendall. It became one of the defining reads of my life. I think everyone should read it. The book has a central theme: Joseph.

Genesis 37.

What I personally find amazing about Joseph's experiences is that I actually think he got it right. Some would say that he was unwise to broadcast his dreams. I think he was right to. We will always have a jealous oppressor if we are audacious enough to dream big. A person will always attract venom from "brothers" if they are prepared to speak about the dream that is in their heart.

I say, *speak it anyway.*

If Father has given a person a beautiful robe, it would be wrong to keep it in the wardrobe. If the person wears the beautiful robe then criticism, jealousy and even actions to try and enslave the said person will come from "brothers".

I say, *wear it anyway.*

It grieves me to scribe the following, but the behaviour of a small minority of fellow leaders in the city has been like that of Joseph's brothers. In my naivety I held the understanding that when God does something spectacular, then fellow leaders celebrate what He is doing. I never, in my wildest dreams, expected the slur, abuse, Facebook activity and vicious attacks that came from other church leaders. In a city with supposed "unity of churches", I can testify that Joseph always has brothers who won't celebrate the dreams spoken of or the beautiful robes worn.

People respond to this situation very differently. Becky really isn't bothered by the negative behaviour of fellow leaders in our area. My team of primary leaders are not interested either. BCC's pastors and ministry directors are not phased in the slightest.

But it really gets to me.

I have been really affected by this – maybe because it has mostly been targeted at me. Maybe it's because I like to deal with things head on and whispering in corridors, backstabbing and two-faced behaviour are my pet hates. Maybe it's because I call a spade, a spade.

I think that this kind of thing does affect the leader very differently to others. I think it is a crying shame that it happens at all. But the reality is, if a person has a dream and is passionate enough to speak of it; if a person has the audacity to fully wear the mantle (robe) that God (father) has given them – then some "brothers" will not behave in the way that we all know they should.

In combating this behaviour I have developed the following strategy.

Firstly, die to self. Dead men don't have feelings. They don't moan. They don't get offended. It was a great revelation when it dawned on me that the mantle is God's and the dreams are His plans. I am merely a servant who is given the simple responsibility to obey what He is saying. If I was not leading this church in this city then the opposition and criticism I receive would not be directed at me. It really isn't about me at all.

Dying to self is a strategy suggested by Jesus (see Luke 9:22-26) that I forgot for a while – but it works!

Secondly, relational leaders are bigger people. I have realised that the best way to have friends is to be friendly. I treasure the relationships that I do have with leaders in my city, nation and nations. I focus on those relationships and not on the bad ones. The worst thing I could do is to become a victim and isolate myself because I don't want to get hurt. I have seen the devastating effects that hurt and isolated leaders can cause. I work hard at networking and meeting leaders. It matters not if leaders are high profile or leading huge ministries. What does matter is that they are relational. Again, Psalm 133 tells me that if I want to be "drowned" in the blessing of God, then I have to be in unity. I am blessed with some sensational friends and I value our relationship immensely.

Thirdly, champion other people's successes. Sometimes, we get so self-absorbed with what is happening in our world that we forget to look at and celebrate what God is doing with others. Whenever I read an article or hear a story of a leader doing great things, I make contact and celebrate their success story. Championing others is characteristic of a kingdom mindset, not an empire mindset. Recognising other people wearing their "robe" and listening to others relate their "dreams" is a great way to live. I'm sure that if Joseph's brothers had told him of their dreams, he would have celebrated with them.

Fourthly, I don't take myself too seriously. It is an immense privilege to be leading such a great church, but really, I am not Billy Graham. Sky News isn't asking for my opinion on things. I have learnt to laugh at myself more than anyone else. It's hilarious how useless I can be and humbling how God has adorned me with this "robe". Sometimes it seems too big for me to wear, but I think He knows more about the dress code than me.

Fifthly, I have decided to model something different. My people and my children do not need to see a "Joseph's brothers" attitude in me. I may not have the authority to challenge and correct what I perceive to be wrong attitudes in others, but I do have the authority to deal with my own attitudes and ensure that I model something different. I do this by speaking well of those who criticise, praying for leaders in my city, realising that it is okay when others don't agree or like the way I do church and by maintaining a sweet spirit, whether in the prison or in the office of Prime Minister.

BACK RIDERS AND PURGING EGO

When I distance myself and look at the growth of BCC in three and a half years from 62 people on that first Sunday to fast approaching 600 people on any given Sunday, there are scores of great stories and several tales of horror that can be told. The disappointments leave painful memories because, as a leader, one knows that the personal outcomes for many individuals could have been very different if they had made different choices.

What is so frustrating is the number of people that miss out because they are "back riders" and "egos in the house". During the journey of repurposing, these two types of people have had to be watched for and dealt with.

Matthew 19 gives us a painful account of Jesus dealing with a "back rider". A young man comes to Jesus with great credentials and desperately wants in on the action. Jesus first talks of not killing someone, not committing adultery, not stealing or lying, honouring parents and loving your neighbour as yourself. The young man, who is a good guy, smiles and informs Jesus that it is "all good" and that he has had this stuff nailed since he was a boy. Then Jesus reveals the "back rider" within him:

"Jesus told him, 'If you want to be perfect, go and sell all your possessions and give the money to the poor and you will have treasure in heaven. Then come, follow me.'" (Matthew 19:21)

WOW!

Jesus has just exploded in the face of mediocrity. Jesus spoke simply and plainly about the cost of following Him and the young man is exposed as a "back rider".

BOOM! The young man walked away.

I have seen this a number of times in the three and a half short years of leading this church. Use your imagination for a moment. A young man turns up one Sunday morning at our Campus: City. He is clean, sharp, has a great young family and you catch his eye as you're preaching. He is taking notes and loving his time in church. A week later you catch him in the welcome area and say, "Hi". Another week later your Welcome Pastors tell you that the young man has filled in a volunteer application form. Eventually, the young man completes Connect and the next Sunday you see him stewarding in the car park and you think to yourself, "I like this guy."

But then comes the challenge of a preach or a conversation with a pastor that reveals the young man has serious marriage problems or something similar. When he is spoken to about this and challenged to do something to help save the marriage, you hit a brick wall and the following day you get an email saying, "We've left."

Or what about the guy who seems so friendly, warm and supportive? For a while, one would consider this person to be a "people person". But what becomes evident is a hidden insecurity where "being liked by everyone" is the primary objective. From our experience, this type of person would propagate (what I've come to call) the "law of grace". This type of person is *legalistic* regarding the "gospel of grace". They take great teaching on grace totally out of its biblical context and then pursue a life of, "I can do whatever I like because I'm in grace." The difficulty is that this warm, friendly person draws innocent, less mature people into their isolated, rebellious attitude. His "disciples" are encouraged not to respond to any type of challenge presented from the pulpit. "You don't need to be baptised if you don't want to ... Tithing is Old Covenant, they are after your money via manipulation..."

What is the deal here?

These people are what I have come to term "back riders". A great church is simply made up of great people. Many a person wants to be part of a great church. But in a great environment consisting of great people doing life together, people are unable to keep the hidden stuff hidden. It always comes to the surface when the discipleship of close proximity occurs.

Leader: be careful of the "back riders". They aren't helping you build, they are building *on the back* of what you're trying to build.

We are not a Sunday church. We do life with people. Things show up quickly. People want to hang out in a great church, but sometimes they don't want to be great themselves. They want to be in the band, but they don't want to deal with the character flaws. They want the opportunity to be on an internship, but don't want to deal with their failing marriage. They want to be a groupie or a follower, an attendee or part of the "in crowd" and yet they don't want to be a disciple of Jesus.

When repurposing church, don't merely gather a crowd, build great people. Don't let people ride on the back of what is going on, create a church that is Clean. Preach the messages that will challenge people to live more like Jesus. Do not merely be a convalescence pool for lukewarm and lethargic Christians. Build people and watch the church be built.

The second type of person is the type that, personally, I find the most frustrating.

The "ego in the house" guy is one who really does look at everything through the filter of self! The great verse in Psalm 84, for me, is the simplest way to help deal with this type of person:

"I would rather be a gatekeeper in the house of my God than live the good life in the homes of the wicked." (Psalm 84:10)

What a great church requires are people who have a heart for the house and are not merely an ego in the house. You can spot "ego in the house" type people a mile off. They are either "stiff-necked

Pharisees" or "melancholic moaners" – both of which eventually evidence different kinds of aggressive attacks.

Our experience has been that the "stiff-necked Pharisee" will simply not agree with any kind of change, unless it is built around what they believe to be correct. This once resulted in a punch up right before I was about to preach on a Sunday morning. Most people thought it was a planned skit. Wayne Gough (one of my Primary Leaders), who received a right hook to the chin, knew it was for real!

The "melancholic moaner" simply doesn't agree with any kind of change unless it is built around their "gift". This is not a fixed rule but, in our experience, this often occurs with musicians and artistic people. They don't say anything face to face, that's not their style, but keyboard at the ready they venomously communicate their thoughts.

I don't think that you can imagine the email I received from one such scenario. Thirty-one pages of absolute, unprecedented opinion about me, BCC and events that had occurred leading up to the email being sent. Everything in the email was egocentric and utterly incorrect. The sender completely missed the heart of the house and manifested themselves as an ego in the house.

It is such a shame when this happens. When repurposing church, do not allow the "ego in the house" to manipulate any activity. Whatever you do, don't give them a stage. Walk humbly and build according to the plan that God has shown you, but never allow charisma to grab the mic – only character should be allowed that privilege.

What we have built into the life of the house is a passion for the house. We do things like "staff swap" where, for a short period, all staff swap roles so that we appreciate what others do. We get to see things from differing perspectives and no one develops a "my ministry" mindset. All ministries belong to the house, not to an individual. The house belongs to Jesus and we are all privileged to be a part of it.

We have a heart for the house, not an ego in the house.

A BCC STORY: STEFFY

I have actively participated and served in church for most of my life. Prior to BCC, however, much of what I did was for the benefit of the previous or current generation. Where was the preparation, the building of the unstoppable force to hand over with momentum? What would the next generation do with what we left them? Up until 2007 I was very conscious that the answer to this question was an institution, a club that happily ticked over and didn't make much of a noise. Desperation to save a city and immediacy in action were absent.

But … Jesus said that He would build His Church!

I have had the privilege of being part of the repurposing and birth of BCC since the beginning. I threw myself into the life that was being injected into the house. I gave my all from the beginning, from knocking down brick walls at 3.00am, to coming to every meeting and event held and hanging on every word spoken by Pastor James – not out of obligation, but because I wanted to be there. Everything that was brought was wise and yet so incredibly obvious and natural – this was how church was meant to be. The unstoppable force was being revealed!

I love my life as a BCCer. I have the privilege of being on staff here, serving my Senior Pastors and I wouldn't want to give my life to anything else. It is a huge and exciting thing to be a part of something that is so much bigger than myself. I have given all of me over to the house of God and I wouldn't have it any other way. My future is wherever God chooses to take me. Right now, I'm doing as I'm told by my awesome God and my phenomenal Senior Pastors – freedom in obedience is a beautiful thing.

I live and breathe BCC. My life is literally full! John 10:10 is a living reality! Breathe City Church is my home.

PART 4 SUITS YOU SIR

When it comes
to church,
all bets are off;
all rules of
engagement
are cancelled.

INTRODUCTION

In this section the fragrance and flair of BCC will hopefully be conveyed to the reader. This section is designed to allow the reader to catch hold of the nature of the journey thus far, giving details from differing perspectives and giving access to the relationships and personalities of both the operation and infrastructure of the church.

BCC has developed in a very intentional way to become an eccentric organisation that is becoming a model across the nation of how to build church with a clear understanding and confidence in what it is to be unique. "Suits You Sir" is designed to let you, the reader, get an inside glimpse into the formation of BCC as it exists today.

It is also hoped that this section will bring practical guides into how to build and manage church, the leaders and the personalities that make church so exciting. Presented in this section will be personal observation and testimony that will reveal the heart, passion and evidence of the amazing thing that Jesus is doing here in Stoke on Trent.

Exodus 25:9 states:

"Exactly as I show you concerning the pattern of the tabernacle, and of all its furniture, so you shall make it."

This section reveals that which God has shown and how BCC has been made accordingly.

FIND THE MODEL THAT SUITS YOU

In a totally different context I once heard a phrase that went along the lines of,

"There is more than one way to skin a cat."

It's a very strange phrase, especially as I think that RSPCA would have something serious to say about it if you began to experiment in order to prove the sentence true. However, I understand the point the phrase is trying to convey and this has led me to begin to imagine what church could look like if I chose a different model than the one I have been used to.

In my opinion we have become very boring, institutionalised and modular in our approach to building church. Everything about it has a "programme" dimension that we centre around a Sunday morning service. The older model has a Sunday 10:30am service (Communion), 6:30pm (Gospel), Tuesday 7:30pm (Prayer), Thursday 7:30pm (Bible study) and so on.

Then we got all "21st Century Church" from around 1990 onwards. For a younger guy, at best I would describe this as an attempt to "dance like me dad". Honestly, much of what "21st Century Church" does is simply a modernisation of "20th Century Church". Just because a church has a video projector instead of the good old OHP doesn't make it 21st Century. A tad of a rant, I accept, but I have lived nearly all my adult life in the 21st Century.

It's all I know.

Yet I find that "21st Century Church" is predominately talked about by a previous generation who have spent most of their lives in the 20th Century.

What is 21st Century?

21st Century is experimental. 21st Century is more than merely thinking outside the box (that again is a tad "dance like me dad"). 21st Century doesn't know that there is a box! 21st Century is breaking all the rules and pushing the boundaries of everything we know. 21st Century, in linguistical terms, is Stem Cell Research, getting our heads around 9/11, the shop front village called the World Wide Web, all crossed with everything we have done thus far. This has merely got us to where we are now.

So let's grab some of that "Sixties" attitude and experiment with everything, especially since everything is allowed. When it comes to church, this simply means all bets are off; all rules of engagement are cancelled. Let's have a look at the 1st Century Church, honour those who have gone before us, learn from their mistakes and refuse to live under the ceilings that they created.

To understand the essence and heartbeat of what great 21st Century Church is, please read my friend, Tom Rawls' book, *Relentless*. He crafts a verbal image of a Church that is expansive, passion-filled, relevant and accessible to the Google Generation. Be inspired.

Rant over.

So when it came to building a city church in a city that isn't really a city but a bunch of towns put together – a 21st Century city church for the 21st Century, led by 21st Century people; a Pentecostal city church in a city where the Pentecostal Church hasn't really broken through – I began to realise that we would be breaking all prima fascia. I began to realise that the only model we had to help was the Holy Spirit and that He would create what He wanted if we had the audacity to follow His blueprint.

BCC, as a model of church, is fantastic in that it's not a copy. BCC inspires the church that wants to be unique and refuses to follow the crowd. BCC is a guinea pig church that, once again upsetting the RSPCA, pleads for God to be experimental with it. BCC is a freak for chasing after the greatest Revolutionary who ever walked the planet, broke all the rules, didn't think like His predecessors, annoyed the religious, agitated the Pharisees and pleased the Father simply by doing what He saw His Father do.

In order to reach and serve a city (that is not a city but a bunch of towns put together), BCC had to become tribal. Being in one place simply doesn't work in our city. We are building a city church in a city with a township mindset.

BCC is, at present, operating from 10 sites across our region. Each site is unique to its ministerial influence and geographical demographic. For instance, Campus: City, the hub of the operation, is where all the administrative activity occurs. It's where all the finances are managed and it's where my office is.

Campus: Meir is on the main road of one of the most deprived areas of our city. It's where we "farm" our young leaders and cut their teeth for frontline ministry. It's where we serve great coffee at great value in a plush environment to a community that can't afford plush coffee. It's where we throw half a million pounds into a building project because no one throws half a million pounds into that community.

Campus: Trentham is a family congregation which is serving a "community that doesn't exist" – a community that has very little community facilities; a community that is the most affluent in our city and yet has continuous stories of isolation, loneliness and mega debt.

I could go on to talk about Cheadle, Fenton, Hanley, Biddulph, Leek, Newcastle and Stronger, but that is not the point. The point is that we broke the rules. Nothing that BCC does conforms to a model. We have a model that has been downloaded by God. Our aim is to be in every ST postcode by 2020.

God only knows how, but BCC has an unquenchable ability to see people get saved and then develop them into outstanding leaders. It is mind blowing to see the volume and quality of leaders being churned out almost weekly. It's like a production conveyer belt! Therefore, it is part of our mandate that we have to build a church that can accommodate many leaders.

Our model of church smashes the 80/20 rule that others say can't be broken. We so don't believe in the word "can't". Thus BCC is punching way above its weight and size regarding its ministerial operation. We have incredible ministries in operation, all with teams that have the ability to lead churches themselves. We have an "attractional" model of church that is overtly missional. This is a church that pretty much never sleeps. It is high delivery in operation with a work/volunteer ethic that would put to shame most multinational organisations. BCC is only for the brave.

Our model of church is extremely expensive, but obscenely generous. People give like I have never seen before. It is absolutely amazing to watch not simply money, but time and effort given abundantly. Our model of church thrives in a city where (apart from a couple of cinemas, pubs and restaurants) pretty much everything closes at 5.00pm.

Therefore our model of church is the social calendar for people. I have often been told not to pack too much into church life, but the truth is that BCCers live for this. BCC *is* people's lives and they give their all for its progress. They are absolutely in love with Jesus and are passionate for His house and wouldn't have it any other way.

I want to encourage others with this thought: when a church and a leader are secure, they don't have to copy another church model. What can happen is that they can allow the Holy Spirit to inspire a blueprint that is unique to the calling and mandate of that church and leader; to be themselves FULLY and enjoy experimenting.

Here are a few pointers we use:

We will never have enough money. How we choose to build church is expensive and we know we'll never have enough money. We are so cool with this. Matthew 25:23 tells of how it could be said to us one day, "Well done, good faithful servant." I really don't want to hear,

"You missed out on what could have been because of money." What amazes me is that in all of this, some might say, reckless way of building church, we have not had one month in three and half years where the bills have not been paid.

Our parish is where God directs us. It has no geographical borders. The parochial parish system of the past is not how we operate. We are simply committed to setting up shop EVERYWHERE!

We follow the opportunity. If eyes are open and feet are ready, it is amazing what opportunities open up to a church. Most of our activity, whether it be campuses or the buildings of ministries, such as CAP (Christians Against Poverty, www.capuk.org), exist because we went with the moment.

We have got nothing to lose. When we first arrived, change had to occur otherwise the church would have died. We had nothing to lose. We have made a conscious decision to maintain this mindset.

We unashamedly use Twitter and the power of the web. Life is moving fast and we want to keep the channels of communication open at all times. Twitter, emails and websites are used to their full extent to communicate to BCCers and our city.

And finally, "He gets all the glory, He gets all the grief." The house belongs to Jesus and we are merely doing what we believe He is saying. We live free from hassle because it is an absolute privilege to be involved.

Our model of church is one not to be copied, but it is there to help inspire others to discover *their* model of church. Some say that BCC is a unique move of God in Stoke on Trent that is not transferable anywhere else. Maybe so. Yet, I am absolutely convinced that "unique" and "eccentric" are the way that Jesus builds church.

Matthew 9 tells a story about how Jesus was attracted to the eccentric shouting of two blind men. The conclusion of the story is that the men received vision and the crowds shouted, "Nothing like this has ever happened in Israel!" I am absolutely persuaded that Jesus is attracted to those who are eccentric enough to shout for vision. I am also convinced that if this occurs then communities of people, cities and even nations will declare, "Nothing like this has ever happened here before!"

When attending a wedding anyone can walk into a Moss Bros. or similar establishment and take a suit off the rail to wear and look really smart at the wedding ceremony. Yet we all know that the person who goes to the tailor and has a made-to-measure suit is the one we all talk about at the wedding, because they stand out and look amazing.

You can be that person we are all talking about. Don't take the suit off the rail when it comes to building church, go to the tailor and get made-to-measure.

Never, *ever*, be fearful of failure. Failure prevents experiment. Experimenting produces new.

BECKY'S STORY

Spring 2007. I can distinctly remember walking down our road in Cardiff one sunny afternoon, taking the boys to a local toddler group. I was doing my best to keep life normal for them, but life wasn't easy. Looking back, it's easy to see that God was starting the rumblings of trying to reposition us. But at the time all I felt was pain, confusion and frustration.

That day I prayed a prayer that I was scared God might answer! I knew that I may not like the answer to that prayer and certainly the answer to that prayer could take me far out of my comfort zone. But I asked God to "get us out of our situation", whatever that meant. I don't think I really believed that God would answer my prayer, especially in such a dramatic way!

I love Cardiff. I used to visit as a child as my grandparents lived nearby. It was my dream to live there, so when I came to choose a university, Cardiff was my obvious choice. I got married in Cardiff, both my children were born in Cardiff and I helped to pioneer a church and a citywide youth programme in Cardiff. I never wanted to move. I loved the city. I loved where we lived. I loved my son's school. I loved and had spent many years investing in the young people of the city.

Why would I want to move from a city that I loved? From a youth ministry that James and I had worked so hard at pioneering and had grown successfully, affecting thousands of young people across the city and region? From a church which we'd helped repurpose and that had a great team who we loved dearly?

Yet, when James asked me one evening, "Why don't we move to Stoke?" the word, "No" did not come out of my mouth as I always imagined it would.

Something had changed and we felt unsettled in church life, home life – everything.

We were ready for a new challenge, for our own "absolutely awesome adventure" and clearly God was trying to reposition us. Two years prior to the decision to move to Stoke, whilst on holiday, I'd felt God say, "It's a new day." I came home from that holiday expecting life to change, improve and to begin to feel fulfilled. But it didn't. Life got tougher and although I tried to stay encouraged, it didn't feel much like a "new day". For two years the "new day" didn't come and I questioned if it ever would.

That two-year journey, which could be the subject of a book in itself, brought us to what is now Breathe City Church. As my boys so rightly say, "It's the best church in the world!"

We left Cardiff empty, having given all we had to the work and ministry. I did not feel ready to be a "Pastor's Wife". The thought made me shudder. What if I started to dress like one? What if I started to look like one? And what if people treated me like one!

One week day when visiting Stoke on Trent to chat to the existing leadership team, I took my youngest son out from where we were chatting into the main auditorium to try and get him to sleep. I stood by the platform and looked out over the seats and asked God if we could really lead this church. I had no great revelation, but just felt really silly! Why would God use me? Why would God use us? Could we really do it? Was this absolutely crazy – moving our family half way across the country, leaving everything we knew and the life that we had planned?

The thing was, we had no choice. Life was over in Cardiff, there was no doubt about that. It was like there had been a death and a funeral. All we had left was God, so if this was the door He was opening then maybe, just maybe, this had been His plan all along.

Our first Sunday in Stoke was 2nd September 2007. I had dressed carefully, so as not to look like a Pastor's Wife. As we stood in front of the congregation, being introduced, I knew we had come home. A lovely couple came straight up to us after the meeting. The lady held my hands and said, "You're here at last! I have prayed for you every day for the last 18 months and sometimes felt like I was going to die. I was in so much pain for you. But you are here now and I know I can go home to Jesus."

The lovely lady was Rosa, someone I'll always aspire to be like. She was with us only six months before she did go home to be with Jesus. Her family and friends said she never would have gone if she hadn't known the church was in safe hands.

It totally amazes me that someone can pray so diligently for someone they have never met. Imagine if she had never prayed, because I'm convinced there were spiritual forces holding us in Cardiff that were causing us to die. There are times through those 18 months when I thought that God would never show up – times of pain and desperation. So as she told me that when she prayed she'd felt like she was dying, my eyes filled with tears, because I immediately knew and understood that it was her intercession that had carried us through those times.

I honestly believe that it was through her prayers, my mother's and perhaps my own feeble prayer that we were released from our situation in Cardiff to be repositioned to the fantastic city of Stoke on Trent.

So we arrived! The then elders who had been holding the fort graciously gave us everything on that first morning and told us to go for it!

I can remember wondering when it would feel like "my church" and "my home", if you like. When would I be able to walk into the kitchen and move things around? When could I redesign the office? When would it feel like family?

Looking back, the first few months were hard, but at the time they were an adventure! There were people who didn't really want us here, but there were people who did. Rosa helped me get rid of my kitchen fear by giving me a bin bag and saying, "Come on, I've been longing to do this. Let's clear the cupboards!" That was great fun, clearing out the past and getting ready for the future.

We met with all the existing department heads. We gave out and talked until we were exhausted. Our last meeting was with the then department head for Dance. At the end of the meeting she said, "Can I pray for you?" Steffy is now working for us full time as James' PA. That one simple request made me feel like family. It was Steffy and I who redesigned the office together.

Looking back, it's funny how God blessed and used those who embraced our arrival. When we eventually found a house in Stoke on Trent, I received some flowers from three girls. I still have the tag that came with them. It reads, "Welcome to Stoke on Trent, we are so pleased you're here." Through no intentional plan I recently realised that all three of those girls are now full time paid staff at BCC, living out their own dreams of serving God. I wonder, if their hearts hadn't been so open, where would they be now?

I can now truly say that BCC is home. Yes, even Stoke on Trent is home! My family and I are enjoying an absolutely awesome adventure that we barely allowed ourselves to dare to dream. I often wonder why we are so blessed.

Is it because we were truly dead that God could use us or was it because we were willing to pay the price (there is always a price to be paid and it often hurts)? Or maybe it is just because we serve a gracious and generous God.

I don't know, but I am certainly enjoying the journey!

A BCC STORY: SARA

Things began to change for us as a family before Breathe City Church was born, but we had no idea that the journey we were embarking on would lead us to the paths we are now on with the people that we walk with. It started soon after the birth of our first child when we were invited onto the leadership to "help out". The church was broken and in disarray. I had seen broken, weak and damaged people cause what I had thought to be a strong, thriving church, become broken by selfishness and self-promotion.

We tried our best, with very limited experience, to support and share the load. Then Pastors James and Becky were introduced. When we sat down with them, with the current leaders, it was very evident that they were on a completely different level. We knew this was right, despite people saying that Paul, my husband, should be the next leader and others being unsettled by the new weight of authority that they carried. We were with them heart and soul from the first meeting. Paul and I were in for keeps. Pastor James stayed in our spare room whilst still commuting from Cardiff. During this time we learnt a great deal as we talked and listened. For Paul, especially, I think this bonded him to Pastor James in a way that nothing will ever break. So there was change! A new heart and passion joined the new décor on the outside with the new leadership and culture on the inside. This was what created BCC for me.

Now? The change doesn't stop. God challenges and changes me at every step and hurdle and I know the answer always has to be "Yes". I am more passionate about God's house, more desperate to call in salvations, more than ever excited about the next generation, more grateful for His grace and exceptionally humbled to be doing life with the phenomenal people I walk with.

JONATHAN AND HIS ARMOUR BEARER

The story of Jonathan and his armour bearer is one that I hold dear to my heart. It is a story that anyone venturing out on the journey of repurposing church needs to read, digest and meditate on in order to grasp the revelation of what God can do when people are with other people, heart and soul. Yes, you will always have people who are with you because of the vision, but having people with you because they are called to be with you makes the journey so much easier and altogether sweeter.

Jonathan (1 Samuel 14) was, like any leader wanting to take a church on a journey of repurposing, frustrated with the lack of movement in the camp. He desperately wanted life to be more than a nap under a pomegranate tree when there was a mission to be accomplished and an enemy to defeat. Jonathan had the audacity to dare to dream and believe that there was an adventure out there for him to be a part of.

Turning to his armour bearer, Jonathan muttered a little about going over to where life might get a tad interesting, not knowing if it would work, not knowing if there would be victory and not really knowing for sure if God would assist. What he did know was that to stay where he was, was not good enough. Someone, somewhere had to do something and be a catalyst for breakthrough.

What is interesting in this story is that the scripture states, "He did not tell his father." I'm discovering more and more that eccentric exploits done for God sometimes don't get the blessing of the former regime. It didn't stop Jonathan from doing it though. Sometimes, seeking permission is the very ceiling that keeps a generation from fulfilling its destiny. Sometimes a generation needs a "Jonathan" to sneak out and get the victory without anyone knowing about it until they hear the noise. Then they will join in and experience the victory also.

The greatest part of this story is not the climb to the enemy, it is not the victory, it is not the breakthrough that Jonathan achieved, but the reaction of the armour bearer to Jonathan's ridiculous idea that the status quo could be changed. The armour bearer utters words that cause the leader of a church going through a journey of repurposing great emotion:

"Do whatever you think is best ... I'm with you completely, whatever you decide."

On embarking on this ridiculously audacious and dangerous journey or even imagining where we would be three and half years later, the greatest thrill to Becky and myself is not the sensational victories that we are experiencing or the breakthrough that is happening. It's the people that we now have in our world.

People that aren't in it because of the vision. People that aren't in it because it's exciting. People that are in it because of us.

The day I phoned Wayne and Deborah Gough to tell them that we were leaving Cardiff was one of the most ridiculous ever. Having worked with Wayne and Deborah for a number of years, but knowing that they lived in Stockton on Tees, the last thing I expected to hear from Wayne that day was,

"Okay, so where are WE going?"

In an instant, he had decided that he and his family were moving to be wherever God was taking Becky and myself. Wayne is my confidant and we have some war stories that make us laugh, cry and thank God for. We have seen people fall by the wayside, but we are living the dream of a Jonathan and an armour bearer, realising that things don't have to be the way they always have been.

People like Paul and Sara Jukes, our Executive Pastors. The first time we met was in a very interesting meeting with the then leadership team of the church we were about to inherit. Little did Paul, Sara or Becky and I realise that BCC would be birthed so sensationally.

Little did we realise the heartache and the pain of slander and lies we would endure together. At that first meeting something supernatural occurred. That Jonathan and his armour bearer moment happened. Paul and Sara literally gave us the keys to their home and we have been doing life together ever since.

The six of us have been terrorising religion, mediocrity and lethargy this last three and half years and we know that we have a lifetime of it to look forward to.

Not forgetting Derek Barker, who is a prophetic statement in our journey that bridges the past and the future. Derek is the only Elder who made the transition. He was part of the eldership that invited Becky and myself to Stoke on Trent.

The others couldn't make the journey of repurposing, but Derek did. I honour and salute this godly soldier. Derek has been through immense personal battles to stay with us on this walk, but has done so and the future will be forever grateful for his commitment to the process.

Armour bearers like the psychotic Tim and Rhi Davies who got up one morning living in Cardiff and the next packed up and shipped up to live in Stoke. They have walked with us and served us with an unprecedented enthusiasm for many years.

Rhi is like a second mum to our boys and, not knowing what the future held, committed to a journey of adventure like none other.

Armour bearers like our staff team who serve like I have never seen people serve. Who have in their contracts "and whatever else is required".

I'm confident to say that I have the greatest staff team on the planet, working alongside our ministry directors and pastors who do a sensational job of loving and inspiring a city.

The great thing about journeying through the process of repurposing is that people do make the transition and repurposing does work. When a person tastes the goodness of their God, they never want to go back. The people in our world make the journey for us – they are the journey!

My encouragement to others is to remember that church is about people. Leaders simply need to lead, not gather. People who are called to be with you will come with you on the greatest journey ever.

A BCC STORY: PAUL

Wow! What an adventure the last three and a half years have been!
Where do I begin? Pastors James and Becky stayed at our house for
the first few months until they moved to Stoke. I remember
discovering that he didn't sleep much! Night after night was a
download of culture, vision, pastoral guidance, more culture,
leadership training and more culture! I was totally blown away and
couldn't believe that we could "be real", say it "how it is",
stop being super-spiritual and simply enjoy the journey!

A day doesn't go by without something happening. The maturity
of the house amazes me, from people having "paddies" and
tantrums to people now learning to listen first and grow
in understanding. It is so refreshing!

My wife, Sara, and I attended various city prayer meetings across
our city and were rather mystified by what God was doing.
When I gave my life to Christ, God miraculously delivered me and
filled me with His breath. I knew God had revived me! Yet, at many
of the prayer meetings they would cry out for revival and my spirit
would shout out from within, "I am revived!" I was frustrated.

Now I feel fulfilled, no longer frustrated but growing and loving being
a part of God's awesome plan for our city – the Church.
I love how BCC works: watching people come into the house,
functioning, built up, sent out, falling in love with Jesus and passionate about their King!

Pastors James and Becky are amazing leaders. We're truly blessed
to have them in our lives. As a family they have helped us to change
our lives forever and we are so grateful.

A BCC STORY: RHI

So why on earth would I move 150 miles from Cardiff to Stoke on-Trent? Why would I get up one morning and decide it's time to move on? Why would I want to put my house up for sale? Why leave a place where I knew the backstreet shortcuts, saving me 10 minutes on my journey time, where I had my friends and family and a city I loved? Why go to a place I'd only heard of through Pastor James which, let's face it, has never had a lot of positive things said about it?

My reason was this: I had a belief that there had to be more to church than that which we so often see. A belief that church should be full of excitement, adventure, love, unity, growth and fun. That it should be a place that helps us to understand, enables us to live beyond ourselves, to discover and utilise our potential, is inclusive, permeable and always welcoming.

With such a belief, when an opportunity arises for an adventure, it has to be taken. I wasn't put on this planet to live comfortably, facing no challenges and floating through life. I wanted the adventure and, as much as it scares me to admit it, I wanted the uncomfortable.

I've had the privilege of working with Pastors James and Becky for eleven years. I've watched their boys grow up and know that, as a family, they live the adventure. I believe they are anointed to lead us in this adventure. I feel privileged to be part of a church that is bouncing, united and brave in stepping above the parapet. I now live in a spacious place with phenomenal people. The journey hasn't always been easy, as things of worth have a cost, but I've seen God's hand on it and I know He has an immense future for BCC – all we need to do is keep saying, "Yes!"

THE ART OF INTENTIONALITY

My father once told me, "You always say something, even if you are not saying anything." I struggled to understand that sentence until we began this journey of repurposing church. I have discovered that it is true. Luke 3 gives three "M's" that every leader wishing to take a church through the process of repurposing must learn to recognise.

"At this time, a message from God came to John son of Zechariah, who was living in the wilderness. Then John went..." (Luke 3:2-3)

The first "M" is MOMENT. The scripture says, "At this time...." What time? The time that God stipulates. All too often we are so fixed into our programmes that if a God-moment appears, we are too busy doing "church" stuff to respond. The process of repurposing church starts when God says so. Are you looking for His *now moment*?

Three and a half years ago none of us knew that this was going to happen. It's not like we had a plan all worked out. Looking back, and please listen to my experience, this journey has so obviously been a God-moment. No one can manufacture what has happened. It is impossible to man-make a journey like this. One simply has to be dead enough to go with the moment, whatever happens. I say "dead" because I believe it to be true. Dead to self. Dead to reputation. Dead to criticism. Dead to opinions. Dead to everything except doing what you believe – in the very fabric of who you are – because God is speaking.

The second "M" is for MESSAGE. I have learnt that "intentionality" is an art on this journey. The message is not what is said on a Sunday. Yes, you can be intentional with what you preach, but I'm not talking about that. BCC is a message in itself. The journey is a message. I am a message. You are a message. Whether we speak or not we are always saying something. We all have a grace story. We all have testimony and we all have a message to convey.

I have also learnt that if God uses you, like He uses BCC, to convey a dangerous, provocative message of challenge and a statement of audacious faith, then some don't want to hear that message. Some refuse to acknowledge, some disagree and some ignore. But be the message anyway. Every church is a message of faith, hope and love to a city or community. Every church needs to discover the nature of that message and then be very intentional in how it communicates, because even when you stand still and say nothing, you're still saying something.

The third "M" is for MOVE. The scripture says that John *went*. I am amazed at how the previous generation seemed to talk continuously and remark, "There are not many fathers" (see 1 Corinthians 4:15). It seemed to me, as I was growing up in church, that every leadership conversation was about this apostolic dialogue. I don't wish to dishonour the previous generation but, from my own experience, they talked about not having fathers to the detriment of actually being fathers to the next generation. It is all well and good having revelation and then preaching on it, but God is looking for a "John" who "went".

We have to be prepared to move when we hear from God.

The dialogue regarding "change" is as frequent as the dialogue about "fathers" in the previous generation. What we mustn't do is talk about change but not embrace change. The journey of repurposing means that a leader has to intentionally bring change – even for change's sake. Change has to become part of the very fabric of the church. Change has to be the only constant. People must get used to it and learn to embrace it. In my experience a church repurposed is a church that can fully embrace change. If a church struggles with change then change is required.

Here are some of the tools that have been utilised to ensure that we have always been intentional.

Say "No". People will always smile if they receive a "yes", but the fruit of who they are is revealed when they receive a "no". Unity is not unity until two parties disagree and still walk together. If "yes" is always in play, it isn't unity that is manifest but agreement. That is why in the initial stages of repurposing I would say, "No" to people. This was simply to see if they were really a part of what was going on. Nearly all the people that left did so because I said, "No."

Say "Yes". This may seem like a slight paradox, but throwing a "yes" into a church environment causes all sorts of problems. What it does is two fold. Firstly, it develops a "Yes Mindset" – that things can be done and we are the people who can do it. Critics very often say that I surround myself with "Yes Men". My answer is, "Absolutely!" I would be very silly to surround myself with "No Men" as nothing would get done and we wouldn't get anywhere. People with a "yes" attitude are essential for this journey.

A "yes" challenges the "Big Idea, No Delivery" person. A person who was here when we first came to Stoke on Trent, who didn't continue on the journey, was very good at bringing grandiose ideas to the table and was a very good talker. Salesmen are great at clinching deals, but that is not what is required on the journey of repurposing. What is required is delivery. After listening to this person talk for about twelve months, I began to say, "Yes" to every idea they had and then lay the responsibility at their door. I brought accountability to the table. Not long after I did this, the person left and I have not seen them since.

Banish the words "can't" and "just". The word "can't" is the architect of an excuse culture. Use "won't" or "not able to at present", but never use the word "can't" because you probably can. Remove "can't" from your vocabulary and all excuses go out the window. The church can begin to believe in itself again and think that it is able to change the world! Impossible becomes possible.

"Just" is a word that diminishes. "I'm *just* a teacher" or "I'm *just* a hairdresser" are phrases that minimise a person in their own eyes. "I am a teacher" or "I am a hairdresser" allows a person to stand fully in their statement and identity. We banned these two words with dramatic effect.

You may think this insignificant. It is *so* significant. How a church speaks is absolutely important. The Bible says, *"From the overflow of the heart, the mouth speaks"* (Luke 6:45) and *"The tongue has the power of life and death"* (Psalm 18:21).

If a church changes its vocabulary, a church changes.

A BCC STORY: ZOE

Once upon a time I was a Sunday morning attendee. I went to church, sang the choruses and had a little daydream during the preach. Then I left to lead a "normal" teenager's life. I never knew what it was to properly follow.

Coming to BCC was a shock! It was like nothing I'd ever experienced before! There was no daydreaming here. Instead, I listened, I took notes, I put God's Word into practice in my daily life and I served in God's house.

As I let God in, life as I knew it was taken apart. Two years on, it is being put back together, piece by piece, in the most phenomenal way. My life is full. My friends are true friends. My inspiration comes from godly men and women who are full on and sold out for God. My desires are godly desires. I live for Him.

Being a BCCer isn't a part-time, Sunday morning role. It is a lifestyle. We are loved for who we are and inspired to become all that we can be.

Normally at this point in a story, "the end" is appropriate. But how can I say "the end" when my journey has only just begun?

PART
5
THE
MECHANICS
OF
CHANGE

A church setting out on the journey of repurposing needs to make clear and bold statements regarding its future, thus giving people the option of whether or not to be a part of it.

INTRODUCTION

I know that there is much written regarding the concept of change, which is all very helpful in the development of frustration – and frustration, to an agent of change, is a friend, not an enemy.

It is from that place of frustration that many a change is birthed.

Without frustration, change will never manifest.

In respect to repurposing church, however, it is my personal experience that there are few models or examples of how to bring about the change required. The following part of this book is dedicated to giving some practical examples of how change was initiated here at Breathe City Church.

In some cases, what is written here may not correlate with your world or even be culturally relevant, but I thought that it might still prove beneficial to document some of the mechanics of change that occurred in our journey.

I meet many a leader who knows what they *want* to change, but fails to understand the mechanics or practical steps to *bring about* the change required. The following, in my opinion, are the five primary steps that were taken that caused change to occur. For us, the journey was swift and necessary. However, if any church is to embrace the change required to repurpose and be ready to minister in the 21st Century, I believe that these five areas need to be addressed.

WHAT'S IN A NAME?

One of the greatest delights in life is to give birth to another. As a bloke I may not necessarily be an authority on this subject, but I think you understand what I mean. To be the parents of two incredible boys is such a thrill. To be a dad is epic!

Becky and I thought long and hard about naming our boys. Their names were to say something about who they were.

Identity IS influence. If a person fails to understand who they are, they may never live in the realisation of who they are designed and named to be.

Throughout Scripture, names are important.

Throughout Scripture, names change as people enter new seasons, new authority and even new revelation.

I don't need to fill my word count with examples of name changes in Scripture as I'm sure you, the reader, can research this yourself.

Since this book is the story of how a church has been repurposed, I would like to scribe our journey of becoming Breathe City Church.

Bethel Faith Centre, at some point in history became Bethel Christian Church & Centre, yet was always casually entitled, "The Bethel".

This is the church we inherited. The name "Bethel", obviously from Genesis 28, gave us much of what we understood God was asking us to build: The house of God. Not merely a "certain place" but an "awesome place".

The first change that we brought in was more than a name change. To recognise and honour the past we maintained a relationship with "Bethel". With an acknowledgement that we were to be a city church we chose the name "Bethel City Church".

I say that Bethel City Church was more than a name change because it was. Through the various legal processes that we had to go through "The Bethel", as a church and charity was closed down and we started, created, birthed a new church and a Company Limited by Guarantee and a Registered Charity called "Bethel City Church".

The people of the church really grasped this new name and "BCC" became their home. They affectionately called themselves "BCCers", showing a strong ownership and recognition of their identity as living stones in an emerging 21st Century cathedral.

BCC became a multi-site operation and we worked tirelessly at establishing "BCC" or "Bethel City Church" as our identity.

However, it was evident to us that history would not let go of "The Bethel". In fact, it was often stated that "It will always be The Bethel."

BCC was a new church with a new future. For two years, as a Primary Leadership Team, we discussed the possibilities of renaming BCC with a new identity that better represented who we were and what God was doing.

Yet "Bethel" was so applicable to us becoming who we were.

Then revelation came as we re-read Genesis 28. One of my associate pastors in a staff meeting simply stated, "What happened in Genesis 28 was more about the PROMISE than the PLACE."

An explosion of revelation erupted right before our eyes.

BCC was to be identified based on the PROMISE, not the PLACE.

We had given birth to a new church with a new future. This new church was alive and vibrant. When both my boys were born, the first sign that they were alive was that first breath.

New birth is identified when it can be evidenced that the child can BREATHE.

BCC was to become *Breathe City Church*.

Having discussed, with unanimous celebration, with the first and second tier of leadership regarding our renaming as Breathe City Church, we set to task on creating a new brand that would demonstrate the reality of who we were as a church.

Breathe City Church speaks of life, expansion and influence. Breathe City Church and its branding is designed to show a new breath of Pentecostal vibrancy. In Genesis 1 we see that the breath of the Holy Spirit hovered. Breathe City Church carries a fresh breath of the Holy Spirit as a new generation of church is birthed.

Breathe City Church is a name that BCCers have eccentrically celebrated and shows that we are very much alive. The phrase that we chose to help us with our branding and communication of who we are is...

... I am alive. I breathe. Breathe City Church.

STEP UP TO THE PLATE - SIGN ON

Written by Wayne Gough, Primary Leader at Breathe City Church

There is something about a great team. It's hard to put it into words, but when you see it in operation you know. It's sort of magical, it creates a sense of expectation, a buzz, if you like. I remember watching my football team crowned champions of their league a couple of years ago. Even watching from the stands you could feel it, see it and sense it. The air was heavy with expectation, common purpose and destiny.

I have been blessed to have been a part of a great team in my church life. I have tasted first hand that feeling of destiny and purpose as I have sought to serve on a team that looks to build a great church and that simply says, "Yes," to Jesus.

I have had the privilege of knowing Pastors James and Becky for two decades now. We have sat up until the early hours dreaming of what great church could and should look like, how we could mobilise an army of God's people to transform a generation and to impact a nation. I grew up hearing stories about how we could fill football stadiums, but these were just words – we never saw it happen, at least not in Europe.

But the dream was there, it's still there and I still believe in it. It needs a great team to see it accomplished and great teams don't just happen. There are requirements to be fulfilled.

Expectations

Great teams have great demands. It's amazing how many people want to be part of a great team, belong to a great church and yet expect it to just somehow fall into their laps. It won't. If you want to be part of a great team there is a price to pay. It costs.

One thing I have learnt being part of Pastors James and Becky's team for the best part of two decades is that it is no easy ride. Anyone will tell you that to be part of a great team will require hard work and sacrifice. It requires you to push yourself, stretch yourself and move out of your comfort zone.

Here's a thought: perhaps the reason we don't have more great churches, the reason why we don't fill those football stadiums, is that we have things too comfy; we become consumers in church rather than activists.

I think that is one of the key lessons I have gleaned from being a part of an expansive team – that we have been called to go, to do, to embrace and grasp opportunities.

I remember once being at *Campus: Cheadle*. It was evening and we were having our new signage erected on the building the next day. All week we had tried to get hold of an electrician to take down an external light fitting that was where we wanted the sign to be positioned. All week we had drawn a blank and I was about to postpone the signage people when I took a phone call from Pastor James.

I sort of guessed what would come next and, lo and behold, my instinct did not let me down: "Make it happen." What followed was several phone calls and appeals on Twitter and Facebook. Within an hour, a passing electrician had removed the light fitting, the signage was erected and I photographed it with me doing a little victory dance around it.

There is a lot to be said for a "make it happen" attitude. When you and the team you belong to have that attitude it is amazing what follows. Things seem to happen and stuff seems to get done.

Teamwork

When we used to dream about what great church would one day look like, the one thing that was missing from my dreams (but has been evident in reality) has been the calibre of those within the team. I am constantly blown away by the quality of the team that has been assembled. I suppose that, if we use the illustration, any great team is made up of great individuals.

We see that time and time again at BCC. I believe one of the great aspects of this is that quality attracts quality. The top football teams attract the top people because they want to play with the best. In building a secure house ingrained with a clear and attainable vision, we have fostered a house that attracts all-stars to the cause. People who will lay down their lives for the cause of Christ, who give not just what they have, but who they are.

Not just that, but great teams are allowed time to develop and become great. I believe one of my greatest strengths is loyalty. I am in this for the long haul, rain or shine. All great teams must have people who will see it through, who will stand, no matter what.

We have seen people shine brightly in the good times when things are going their way, only to come unstuck when things don't go as they had planned or how they wanted. Now you're thinking, "Do you have a football analogy for this Wayne?" Well, yes I do! You know the sort of "Prima Donna" who kisses his badge one minute, only to put in a transfer request the next?

That is why to be a part of Pastors James and Becky's team, your character is of far more value than your gifting. That's why we are building a team that can be stretched, who when they suffer disappointments bounce back on their front foot.

Finally, one aspect Pastors James and Becky excel in is bringing through new talent, allowing space for people to come through. It sounds simple, but is often a stumbling block for many churches and teams. We need to strike the right balance between loyalty and causing a bottleneck. At BCC we have created a spacious environment where people can come up through the ranks. One of the key components to this is allowing people to realise that who they are is far more important than what they do. That way, we do not try to protect our empires, but rather celebrate when people succeed us.

Honestly, it works and it is a joy to see. It keeps the team fresh, vibrant and yet full of wisdom.

Leadership

Finally, and perhaps the most obvious of all, great teams need great leadership. I believe everything rises and falls on leadership. Strong leadership produces strong teams, godly leadership produces godly teams, and you need both to excel for the King and to stay true to the vision, direction and purpose that God has given you. Perhaps the greatest complement I can pay my Senior Pastors is this: no matter what happens, no matter what the cost, it's all about Jesus. It has to be or it is all pretty pointless.

No matter how clear your vision, how strong your leadership style or how committed your team, if Jesus is not at the centre it's all for nothing. *"Unless the Lord builds the house those who labour, labour in vain"* (Psalm 127:1).

I cannot tell you how much I have benefited being part of a great team, on a great journey, building a great church for a great God. It has been hard, difficult, stressful and yet always rewarding, fulfilling and exhilarating.

I mean what is the alternative? A boring life?

No thanks!

PICK LIST

From what I understand, a *revolution* (taken from the Latin *revol-tio* meaning "a turn around") is a comprehensive and fundamental change in government or organisational structure. I also understand that, even though there may be holistic planning that is put into the preparation, a revolution tends to occur in a relatively short time frame.

I am also aware that in any revolution, whether it is political, generational or spiritual, there is also a common thread.

Every revolution has a sound.

Or song.

Having been in church from an early age, I am also very aware that many of the controlling issues or wrestles or opinion formers have a strong tendency to gather around the subject of the sound of the house.

The song.

Music.

Oh yes!

The reality is, every revolution has a sound.

Every generation has a sound.

Every church has a sound.

When we look globally at the influences regarding corporate praise and worship we see a hugely diverse spectrum of amazing leaders in this field. Through the decades that I have had the privilege of being involved in praise and worship bands, there have been so many waves of style, fragrances, personalities, teaching and expressions. No wonder a church can get confused.

If a church is to be redefined it has to discover its own sound.

Obviously, every church is influenced by others but the Senior Pastor IS the worship pastor and has to clearly know what the sound of the house should be.

Psalm 144:9 is the primary scripture that, I believe, began to reveal the sound of Breathe City Church:

"I will sing a new song to you, O God!"

That simple.

Breathe City Church was to be a church where the new song was to be sung. The reasoning behind this is that when the "new" song becomes a part of who we are, then "change" would not need to be a necessity for the next generation; change becomes the natural constant.

The next generation would not have to experience what we had to experience in bringing change. Change would be in the fabric of the church.

To set the scene...

... The first Sunday service that I experienced was one of the most unusual I had ever seen. I have no doubt that the musicians were godly people who loved Jesus. What I will say was that it was a strange affair.

For any church to develop its "sound" there are four absolute ingredients required.

The Leader

As already stated, the Senior Pastor has to be the worship leader. I'm not saying they have to function in this role – we have to distinguish between leadership and ministry.

The ministry of this role can be delegated. The leadership has to be established.

All too often a worship pastor, or music director, is leading this ministry in the direction they believe it should go. The preferred influence or preference of the worship pastor is then brought into the life of the house and culturally this creates an issue.

The Senior Pastor will most definitely know the sound of the house that he requires. If the Senior Pastor is leading the process there will always be hostility, confrontation and a power struggle, but it is imperative that the ingredient of leadership is established.

Senior Pastor, what do you believe is the sound of the house that God has entrusted to your leadership?

The Standard

Again a contentious issue, but excellence has to be an ingredient that is added at the outset. However, we are not instantly going to be on par with Hillsong or Planetshakers. There is a process.

Our process was quite simple:

Develop a pick list: we chose 20 songs that we were going to use for the next three months (this itself caused issues, even though I only chose 10 of the 20).

I required that all the musicians learnt the music so that no sheet music was required on the stage.

We booked a day to meet when all of this could be explained to anyone who was in the church who wanted to be involved in music.

The results were amazing. The then worship pastor left. New musicians who were not a part of the clique emerged. People who really were not cut out for public ministry demonstrated that they were not cut out for public ministry.

We have now moved on to a place where all our vocalists and musicians are required to have professional lessons and learn, to a proficient standard, at least one other instrument.

The Stage

It's not just about the music. As a generation we have so much visual stimuli it is incredible. Have you ever stopped and looked at the stage in church?

The sound has a look.

I knew that our sound was to be energetic, alive, exuberant and even eccentric. Static, intense, dare I say miserable looking was not what our sound was to look like.

It was a great joy to work with the "musos" and engage in a journey where they began to enjoy, smile, laugh, even laugh at themselves, love praising Jesus and love leading people in praise.

You know when musos are enjoying themselves – their faces tell you!

The Attitude

What is in will come out. Character is always way more important to me than charisma. In order to discover a person's attitude, give them an opportunity.

We did this in a very expensive way that I would not advise others to do, but it is a great illustration. It is great because we got away with it, but it could have been disastrous.

We did a live album.

We got away with it because we broke even, financially, and it was a good debut album.

Firstly, we asked people to write songs. Secondly, we then created arrangements for the songs that had been written. Thirdly, we asked for the rights of the songs to be handed over to BCC (this was a legal process). Fourthly, we chose carefully who would be on stage during the live recording.

Without a shadow of a doubt, this broke the camel's back and I truly discovered that what happens in private always comes out in public.

The emails and slanderous comments where outrageous. The back-lash was incredible.

And it was so worth it!

Every Sunday as the church gathers, I stand amazed at the absolute transformation that has occurred. It is sensational. It is genuinely the outworking of that which I believe God has revealed to me regarding the sound of the house. The musos are such an amazing example of how redefining church for future generations is possible. The joy of testimony after testimony of people being healed in the praise and worship, the amazement of people getting saved who danced on drugs and now dance in the presence of God in the company of His people. The "X factor" of the church where "the bounce is in the house" is a sight to behold.

The passage of Scripture from Ezra 3:10-13 best articulates what I'm trying to communicate:

"When the builders completed the foundation of the Lord's Temple, the priests put on their robes and took their places to blow their trumpets. And the Levites, descendants of Asaph, clashed their cymbals to praise the Lord, just as King David had prescribed. With praise and thanks, they sang this song to the Lord: 'He is so good! His faithful love for Israel endures forever!'

Then all the people gave a great shout, praising the Lord because the foundation of the Lord's Temple had been laid.

But many of the older priests, Levites, and other leaders who had seen the first Temple wept aloud when they saw the new Temple's foundation. The others, however, were shouting for joy. The joyful shouting and weeping mingled together in a loud noise that could be heard far in the distance."

BOLD STATEMENTS

What I knew was that I had to make bold statements. I had to be cheeky enough to lay out the carpet so that not only the spiritual realm knew, but also people knew that we were not merely here for a season only to be gone the next. A church setting out on the journey of repurposing needs to make clear and bold statements regarding its future, thus giving people the option of whether or not to be a part of it.

Within four months I called a "Vision Sunday" that would map out the next 30 years of activity in this church. It was to be defiant and accurate. It was a day I will never forget. People turned up from all over the place. The building was packed. People were noisy. People were ready to heckle. People wanted me out. People even hated me, but I was adamant that a line in the sand had to be drawn and I was pumped for the occasion.

Below are the headlines and some description of the vision and dreams I had for Breathe City Church.

Our VISION was to be as simple as I could make it:

BUILDING A CHURCH THAT LOVES PEOPLE FOR WHO THEY ARE AND INSPIRES THEM TO BECOME ALL THAT THEY CAN BE.

This was based on some lessons that God had led us through. For instance, the stories of Abraham, Isaac and Jacob were huge lessons. We had to ensure that BCC was *generational*. We already knew that the passage of scripture from Genesis 28, the story of "certain" to "awesome" was drastically important. I was also convinced that I had to publicly make the statement that we were to be a hard working church and not one that sits, prays and waits for revival. We were going to get our hands dirty and do all that we could to feed, clothe and serve our city. This was taken from Matthew 14:16 where Jesus says, *"You feed them."*

There were other things that I highlighted. For instance, the statement in Zechariah 4:2 where the question is asked, "What do you see?" I was fully persuaded that God was asking us what did we see, not what had been seen in the past or what was the general viewpoint of today.

I personally saw a 21st Century cathedral – this is what BCC is fast becoming.

Finally, from Exodus 4:2 I was convinced that God was asking the question, "What is in your hand?" I was of the understanding that the resources required were already in our hands.

Alongside all of this was the research that we had carried out during our FOD walk three months earlier.

Then I laid it out in a very plain fashion.

Following are the notes from which I communicated all that I know God had put on my heart. With fear and yet an absolute godly confidence, I stepped out to speak to a bunch of people that I hardly knew, who hardly knew me, and uttered a statement that most of them didn't stick around long enough to see was true or not. This book is evidence that God knew what He was doing and we live in the reality that Jesus IS building HIS church.

What I see (Vision)

Building a church that loves people for who they are and inspires them to become all that they can be.

By 2020 we'll see a church that...

By 2030 we'll be a church that...

By 2040 we'll pass on a church that:

- Glorifies God and breathes life into Stoke on Trent
- Is a distribution centre
- Has localised centres of mission and ministry in every city post-code
- Has national/international centres of mission and ministry
- Jesus is proud of (as a groom is of his bride walking down the aisle)
- Reaches and serves the city and residents practically, emotionally and spiritually
- Is pioneering and experimental
- Is large and influential
- Is generational
- Is mature regarding church government and leadership structure (note: work of Holy Spirit)
- Loves God and loves people
- Is modern and has the spirit of excellence
- Is full of life and vitality (new song)
- Is clean, generous, honouring, positive, healthy, secure and true
- Is a household name in Stoke on Trent
- Has recognised, anointed leadership
- Is a house of prayer/fasting (tap into power)
- Has great specific ministries/departments
- Answers the cry of the city (no such word as "can't")

Condensed...

A church that is building, *numerically*, to a strength where Stoke on Trent has to recognise our influence; *strategically*, to a standard where others will follow our model; and *generationally*, to the level that we are already planning succession 30 years from now.

Purpose

Denominational Purpose: to give every man, woman and child the opportunity of understanding the gospel and to provide a church where they can grow and develop in ministry for the glory of God (Assemblies of God).

Local Purpose
BCC exists to bring glory to God and to breathe life into the city of Stoke on Trent

Culture/Values
Clean, Generous, Honour, Positive, Health, Secure and True

Attitude
"Well done good and faithful servant." (Matthew 25:21)
   WELL: Excellence by choice
   DONE: Whatever it takes
   GOOD: Right practice
   FAITHFUL: Pleasing to God
   SERVANT: Called to serve

I believe that this gave no room for confusion as to what we were to become. It was clear and in print. Any church that is to go through the process of repurposing must not be apologetic and embarrassed, but absolutely up front and transparent in its vision of the future.

People must know that what was, is not going to be what is to come. We are still very much on target to achieve that which we believe for. It is still an incredible journey. Now, as then, people disagree with our strategy and philosophy. In fact, one Christian leader recently emailed me the following:

"As you are aware, I've heard various criticisms from some other local church leaders directed at BCC ... predatory, arrogant, superior, controlling etc."

I totally appreciate that it isn't everyone's cup of tea, but a leader who is building must be convinced of what God has laid upon his heart.

I am.

PRAY MEN!

If church is serious about repurposing and a leader is committed to the process, then there is one sure way to tell. The single and most obvious sign is that the men pray.

Church is, for blokes, very often considered painful at the best of times. Yes, we'll sing on the terraces, but it's not the same in church. We'll chat to people we don't know in the pub, but it's not the same in church. We'll confront an issue in the workplace, but it's not the same in church.

The Church, in general, has become a woman's domain and for a church to rise up, to go on a journey of repurposing, the blokes have to lead the way.

One of the things I love about BCC is that "blokes are blokes"! It's a "man's church".

One of the first things that I did was get all the men into a room (then about 20) and say that from now on the blokes of the house were going to lead the way. We were to start a night of prayer on a Friday night with the bribe that if they came then we'd go into town in the early hours for a curry.

Most of the men who were in that room that day didn't make the journey, but what an amazing men's night of prayer we still have every month. The curry is good too. Not only do we have Prayer, Laughs & Curry (PLC) every month that is attended by 30-50 blokes, but we also meet to pray every Sunday morning from 6.00-7:30am.

I'm not talking about flag waving, "I have a picture," type prayer meetings. I'm talking about prayer meetings that blokes enjoy. We have a laugh, we pray in our normal day to day speech and we see answers to prayer. I don't know what the upper room was like, but I imagine that the disciples were not effeminate! I imagine, as most were fishermen, that it was an environment where blokes were blokes.

No wonder we have so many young women come to our church, because the blokes are blokes. Anyone looking for a godly warrior is obviously going to come to BCC and have a look. Sold out, on fire, non-compromising men of God cause a church to be explosive. Interestingly, the married couples where the man hides behind the woman never last long at BCC. Either the man puts the trousers back on and brings his A Game to the house of God or they leave.

Ahab doesn't live here any more, but there are plenty of Daniels, Joshuas, Peters, Pauls, Stephens and James'.

James 5:15-16 tells us that the prayer of a righteous man is effective. It talks about how Elijah was a man, just like you and me. There is something powerful when normal, righteous men pray. The church comes alive. They sing in church like they are on the terraces. They talk to people they don't know, like in the pub and they confront what needs to be confronted like they do in the workplace.

We banned tambourines, flags, banners, ribbons and all that other stuff that makes a bloke's stomach churn. We made the church "bloke friendly" and guess what? Not only are we seeing unsaved husbands get saved a plenty, not only are blokes bringing their friends to church who get saved, and not only are blokes really enjoying being in church – but the girls of the house LOVE it!

Straight-talking and no super-spiritual mumbo jumbo. Real people loving a real God reaching a city in real ways. Simple. Powerful. Effective.

Don't get me wrong. It hasn't been easy getting to this stage. It is incredible how much moaning men can do when they have lived in the house of Ahab for so long. I have seen some of the most pathetic and immature behaviour. But as a leader I must front up and sometimes simply ignore such petulant activity and press on.

Respond to the blokes who are rising up. Spend time with the "sons" of the house and refuse to capitulate. Appoint strong men to positions of leadership and have fun.

I can't stress how important this is.

The men of the house must be encouraged to be men and released to live the adventure in God that they were designed to live. As soon as a man is born they get put in a cot. When they grow out of that they get put behind a desk at school. Then they get a job and get put in a 9-5. Then they get married and put in a two-up two-down. Then they die and get put in a coffin. Men are put in boxes their whole lives, but they are designed to live free, pursuing the wild adventures that God has got before them.

We encourage all the men to read things like, *The Barbarian Way* by Erwin Raphael McManus, *Wild at Heart* by John Eldridge and *Diamond Geezers* by Anthony Delaney. We challenge all the men to do the corporate fasts that we do, whether that be for 3, 7, 14, 21 or 40 days. The men are encouraged to lead the way.

We have physical ministries like *Lovestoke* that require manual labour in restoring and decorating houses or rectifying playgrounds. We get the men helping in the practical and the public, ministerial settings and being as comfortable in both.

Don't let a Gideon stay hiding away. Don't let a David stay carrying sandwiches to his brothers. Don't let a Moses continue with a stutter. Don't let an Elijah wish he were dead. Don't let a Peter remain a Cephas. Don't let a Thomas live in doubt. Don't let a Paul remain in Barnabus' home.

Empower the men and watch the house prosper.

A BCC STORY: BEN

My Breathe City Church story began in October 2007 during the "Cultural Revolution". I was six weeks into a yearlong internship with the church following three years as a student in the city. My world began to change immediately. Nothing could have prepared me for what was about to take place and yet strangely everything inside of me was ready to jump on board.

It has now become the ride of my life!

It was as if, suddenly, I had woken from the most incredible of dreams only to discover the dream was in fact a reality. For many years I had dreamt about a church that was alive, vibrant, expansive and one that not only exists for the sake of existing, but exists to impact a whole city, even an entire nation!

I consider it a privilege to have been on this amazing BCC journey from the very beginning. However, I have been overwhelmed by the quality of people who have been added since then. There is nothing more exciting than watching someone embark on this journey for the very first time, taking small steps at first then progressing in giant leaps into their God-designed future.

It did not take long for me to realise why BCC is here and, perhaps more significantly, why I am here. BCC exists for the next generation, for those who are not yet part of the house. I am here for the house. There is no greater joy for me than being part of this house alongside some sensational people. I now have the privilege of taking part in someone else's story and they are now a part of mine. My life is no longer my own, because I now belong to the house.

A BCC STORY: JASON

My family and I have been a part of BCC pretty much since the beginning. It is a dangerous, out of your comfort zone, challenging church – which is what I like!

People's lives are passionately committed to Christ. You are inspired to be all that you can be and the BCC "Bounce" is something else!

The Connect course got me pumped and plugged into the heart of the church and what it's all about. Since then I've had the honour and privilege of serving alongside the most awesome and "real" people.

BCC exists to love and inspire and shout out the message of Jesus to our city. The journey in three and a half years has been fast, full and full-on. And this is just the beginning.

EPILOGUE

The journey from a beach hut to a palace has been sensational.

It has been humbling to see what God can do when people say, "Yes," to Him.

It has been exhilarating to see so many lives radically transformed by the power of the gospel.

It has been a privilege to be involved in the emergence of a city-transforming church in my home city.

It has been everything I ever dreamt that redefining church for future generations would be.

It has been an adventure that I hope and pray encourages others that Jesus is still building His church.

It has been!

What I realise is that we have merely crossed the starting line. As a church we have been put in a privileged position ready to effect the future. What I am recognising is that it would be easy to stay here basking in the success of what "has been" in the last three and a half years. But the thing is, if we now stand still, by default, we will be going backwards.

The Bible says that,

"The Kingdom of God is forcefully advancing and forceful men lay hold of it." (Matthew 11:12)

Thus, we have to keep going and keep advancing.

If we don't we reproduce the same scenario, if we stay here, then the next generation will have to go through the same process. The whole reason for this experience is not merely to create a model of repurposing church. It has occurred so that we have a head start and are able to give the next generation something to build upon.

What was quoted at the beginning of this book still applies:

"Hats off to the past, coats off to the future."

Yesterday we experienced what it was to repurpose church.

Today we have written about it.

Tomorrow is yet to be experienced, but it is full of people desperate for a Saviour. Tomorrow is rammed with potential to see a city transformed. Tomorrow is an opportunity for His Church to be mobilised to effect change and bring glory to God.

What we have done has merely brought us to where we are. To move and advance into our future we have to learn how to lead such an awesome church. We need to learn from those further along the journey. We need to consistently enquire of the Lord and not presume that we know how to operate. We need to empower the releasing of the next generation of leaders and followers.

A leader that I greatly admire and whose friendship I deeply appreciate, Pastor Andy Elmes, prophesied the following over BCC:

"I saw a church in the future, a church that had a lot of glass to it, a church that stood out and it was almost iconic and it was a church that none of you have yet imagined, but God imagined before you even set out upon this journey.

I saw a banner upon that church that said Ephesians 3:2, 'Unto Him who is able to do exceedingly, abundantly, far above all you can ask, imagine or think or dream in your wildest dreams.'

And God is saying to you, 'I challenge you on this day, that if you go to the very boundaries of your imagination, the very stretching point of what's possible, I'll always meet you there and say, "Have you had enough or do you want some more?" Know that you'll never catch up with me.'

And God says, 'As far as you'll run I'll always be ahead. You've got to spend the currency of your days with excitement, passion and big dreams.'"

To which we say, "Amen!"

Our story continues...